LIFE LESSONS LEADING TO SUCCESS

by

Angeline Benjamin

LIFE LESSONS LEADING TO SUCCESS

Success is when you are happy with your life,

and you have achieved what matters most to you.

True happiness is when you realize that your gratitude

lies in what problems you don't have

rather than complaining about your problems.

Angeline Benjamin

My dear friend Adaobi Bakare
It is such a pleasure
being able to meet you in
person... you are an
Inspiration.
I hope you enjoy reading
this book as much as
I wrote it.

Angeline Benjamin

Accolades

"Angeline shares the valuable 'Life Lessons Leading To Success' she learned from her parents. It is absolutely a 'Must Read.' They wanted her to be herself and not a counterfeit! They wanted her to take action! They gave her unconditional love, guidance and support and empowered her to attain Success. The rest was up to her! Angeline now encourages the reader to succeed by inspiring us to live the best life! Congratulations Angeline, thank you for sharing your Life Lessons!" Joan E. Wakeland

"I've had the true privilege of knowing Angeline since she joined my Heart Link Network for entrepreneurial women five years ago. She always impresses me with her high integrity, her giving spirit and her sound advice. She sees what you may not see in yourself. Angeline is a mentor who has challenged me to stretch my capabilities and accomplish goals that I may not have ever completed or even considered. When Angeline asks you to do something, do it and you will see results!" Caprice Crebar

"I have known Angeline for about 4-5 years now and in that time, I have seen her transform from a rather shy individual into someone who repeatedly challenges herself and stretches beyond the limits and restrictions we sometimes impose upon one's self that hold us back. In addition, she has encouraged others along the way and is always available to help or offer her assistance. She is a very caring person, and it shows through in her words and actions. She truly has stepped out of her comfort zone into an amazing Entrepreneur that I am proud to call my Associate and friend." Catherine Barr

"ANGELINE BENJAMIN, is a woman who definitely cares about the growth of women (and men too) in their business adventures!
She goes out of her way to help others at all times, and with her vast knowledge in business over the years she knows exactly where to direct others to and how to make connections. If you have Angeline in your business corner you can feel very privileged!" Nanciann Horvath

"Our credibility rises up from what we know. What we know is what we have experienced. Angeline's journey is a perfect example of that. Each step of the way starting with her parents, she has been guided and mentored and remains to this day open to that. She is so passionate about how she followed those directions, she has come to understand the importance of

mentoring for others to support them in their journey as well. Out of that has come a business and career as a high impact coach and now an author. This book is full of connections for people from all cultures, backgrounds, and experiences. This is a resource for everyone wanting to go places and accomplish their missions. Angeline is a professional with integrity and I highly recommend you get to know her and access her gifts just as she has both personally and professionally. A great read and looking forward to more of this beautiful journey as it unfolds . Great work Angeline." Laurie H Davis, Founder, Author and CEO of Self Worth the Missing Link EST 1997

Having worked with Angeline for many years both as a colleague and supervisor, I know her to be a dedicated, loyal, and sincere professional. A consistent strong work ethic focused and committed to her tasks complimented with a contagious positive attitude has always been Angie's unique style! During her tenure Angie was strategic in establishing strong Restaurant Food Safety systems and overall restaurant Food Safety culture. During those same years, external to the company Angie's influence was broad working with Federal, State and Local health agencies specific to Food Safety Regulation and substantive issue resolution. Angie's passion, confidence, and sincere approach to working with others, often in very tenuous circumstances, gained her the respect and appreciation of those with whom she interacted. I have often seen and respected Angie's personal passion and commitment to personal goals and family. Her ability to balance very responsible work responsibilities while being true to herself and family never wavered, this takes dedication, character, and personal strength on many levels! We can all learn from Angie's example. In this book of life lessons, Angie's recounting of her family history, education, careers, and personal life tell a consistent theme which we can all benefit from by our own personal refection. I encourage you to complete the "Questions to Empower You" at the close each chapter! Becky Stevens-Grobbelaar, Director, Food Safety & Regulatory Affairs (Retired 1/1/17)

"Angeline is a true treasure. Our subconscious mind gives guidance if we choose to listen. I recall meeting Angeline and telling myself this is a person I want to know more about. Many of us look at the Corona Virus as what we can't do. The virus has offered me the time to reach out to those people I always wanted to talk to but never had the time. In our meeting, we discussed the Gallup Strengths and it was fun connecting to parts of me that are inherent joys and strengths. If you are asked to spend a one to one with Angeline—follow your subconscious clue you will be glad you did." Rosalyn Kahn, Author, Speaker, Coach, College Professor, and Entrepreneur

"The difference between someone who is successful or not isn't usually capabilities, it is the ability to believe in their capabilities. There's a myth that successful people are born with an abundance of self-confidence--they just knew early how good they were. In reality, some of the most skilled people in the world start out with significant self-doubts. The difference is that they take the time to learn self-confidence. I love this book, "Life Lessons Leading to Success" because it breaks down life's lessons that led the wonderful, thoughtful author to succeed." LuAn Mitchell, President Big Media USA

"Angeline is truly a remarkable woman. She had a long and dedicated career in the food industry and has now dedicated herself to the betterment of women specifically and humanity at large!
"Angeline Benjamin did a brilliant job in writing this book by sharing her family life as well as business challenges and successes. What I especially liked was at the end of each chapter she asks the reader to reflect and answer questions for themselves that will inspire and empower as well as being thought provoking. This for me is quite valuable and applicable to daily life. I highly recommend this book." Dr Iris Rosenfeld

"She has been a faithful and steadfast friend and an inspiration to all those whose life she has touched! Congratulations on this new endeavor of authoring your first book!" Barb Knapp-Colston

"This book reflects Angeline Benjamin's cheerful and inviting nature. She drew me in immediately with her authentic stories and the lessons woven throughout them. The questions at the end of each chapter are personal and thought-provoking. This is an excellent book to give or recommend. Angeline is an accomplished woman. She enjoyed a successful career, is now an entrepreneur and a world traveler. Angeline is someone who really loves and understands dogs. Her dogs are her children. I always enjoy staying with her dogs. I find them well trained, well behaved, and well loved." Kathy Elliot

"Angeline Benjamin is a great mentor and a good friend of mine. I am so proud that she is publishing her book and it's an absolute honor to write about her as a true friend and a community leader. A great quality about her, is that she is very straight forward and direct. Another great quality of

Angeline is that she is very punctual and always meets her deadlines. She is compassionate and takes her work very seriously. She gives every client personal attention and very diligent in her work. I really love her as an Accountability coach and would love to work with her in future. She will provide great value in her book, which is mainly dedicated to her parents. Love to read her book." Karabi Banerjee

A Tribute to Angeline
and Life Lessons Leading to Success

There have been a few experiences in my life that have given me great purpose and blessings. This book is one of them. When I wrote my first book, I had no idea I would develop a passion for helping others get their stories on paper and then published in books. Angeline's story has inspired me, it has helped me get to know her on a deeper level, and it will also do these things for you! Her story is of courage, determination, and conviction.

Her life's mantra became a common theme in this book, as she would say, "What do I have to lose?" Anytime she faced a challenge, she said it, and you can learn from her to say it too! When you think about it, what do you have to lose? It is worth it to overcome challenges, live your life, give it your best shot! Don't look back, take chances, overcome what gets in the way; it makes your experiences so much more rewarding.

When we started on this journey, it was pre-COVID. We could have been like some and made excuses about why we couldn't get this book done. If you know Angeline, you know excuses are not in her vocabulary. Some might have said, "The plan we had won't work if we can't meet in person." Sure, we could have waited, we could have given up. We both are alike in this way if plan A doesn't work, look for a Plan B. Giving up was not an option.

That is what I love about Angeline; she doesn't give up on her goals. You will find out many things about Angeline when you read this book, but the common thread was never giving up on what she wanted in her life. As she describes her life stories, she honors her parent's influence on her out of her love and devotion to them.

Angeline's story is that of determination, tenacity, and grit. Life is sometimes more about the journey than the result. It is not an easy path when we overcome challenges, but who needs easy! In this case, we had both an amazing journey, and the result was getting Angeline's story in print.

We hope that you will be inspired to take action in your life. Find the resources you need, and think outside the box to get what you want. Look for mentors and coaches to help you along the way. Angeline would be the first place I would look. I have heard that if you don't believe in yourself, find someone who will believe in you! Angeline can be that person for you. Stand on her shoulders if you need confidence and want to accomplish something extraordinary. Through Angeline's stories, it is my hope and prayer that you feel like you can conquer the world or at least any challenge that comes along the way. Please don't give up on your dreams, live them out by accomplishing one goal at a time.

I thank Angeline from the bottom of my heart for trusting me to go on this journey with her. It has brought me so much joy to be a part of getting her story to you!

Lori Raupe

Dedication

This book is dedicated to my parents.
I am very grateful for their impact on my life.
Their unconditional love and sacrifice
allowed me to flourish in life.
I honor them by living my best life.

Contents

Foreward
Robbie Motter

I first met Angeline Benjamin at one of my monthly networking meetings in Southern California. The moment I met her, I knew that she was destined for bigger things. I could also see in Angeline's determination and a desire to succeed.

From her corporate career, she already had been training staff and speaking worldwide for many years. With all this expertise, I knew she would make an expert action coach and speaker. I also thought she should tell her story and write a book to share her life experiences. As we talked about it, she asked me if I would be her mentor, and I said, "yes." As her mentor, all I really had to do was be her cheerleader and make sure she kept moving forward. With all her determination for this new career, my job was easy. I helped her step out and step up to greater heights and asked her to run one of my networks as a director and be a co-director of an additional group. She said "yes" to both. She was easy to mentor as she was eager to learn everything about being an entrepreneur.

Since she had retired from the corporate world, she had a passion for making a difference and helping women. Her objective was to become a very successful entrepreneur, which she has done. As I got to know her more, I learned the story of her amazing life where she never gave up and accomplished so much. I started encouraging her to write a book on her life as her legacy, have a television show, and start offering her services as an action coach. She has done this, and she has been doing all of these things very successfully. Her first response to me about the book was that she did not like to write, so I told her to record her words and find a great writing skills coach. I then recommended she connect with Lori Raupe, a very talented coach who herself had written many books and had all the skills to help Angeline make this dream happen. Their connection was a great collaboration, and the rest is history. As this book is done, Angeline is already thinking of another book she can write to inspire, educate, and empower her readers.

In Angeline's book, you will be inspired by an incredible story of resilience and adaptability as a young 18-year-old girl traveled from her home in Indonesia with her beloved sister to her new home in America. Together they found a new culture, new experiences, a new language, and people that supported them. She found what all American's hope immigrants find here, opportunities for dreams to come true.

Angeline is proud to be an American and has lived a life of success and accomplishments, all of which have inspired me. You will also be motivated as you learn from Angeline's internal compass; her true north is success in everything she endeavors to accomplish.

I am excited that you are about to embark on this journey with Angeline, an action coach, who's desire is to teach through her impactful stories. As you apply the principles in Life Lessons Leading to Success, you will be encouraged to reflect on your life lessons and learn to become a better version of yourself.

Introduction

Thank you for taking the time to read this book. It is my hope that my life lessons inspire you to take action! I wrote this book for several reasons, the first is to honor my parents. The influence they have had on my life and the lessons they taught me were the first and most important of the many people whose mentoring made a difference in my life. Their efforts and education, along with my experiences, have created the success I enjoy today. The question for you is what is in my stories for you? I urge you to learn and apply what you read. I hope my life inspires you, empowers you, and educates you to take action. Don't waste your life, grow into the person you want to be.

My parents instilled in me the confidence to be myself, trust myself to do the right things, and be responsible for my actions and success. My father modeled a life where he was an entrepreneur and followed his passion. I am so grateful for their impact on my life and the sacrifices they made to allow me to flourish in life. At great sacrifice, they sent my sister and I to the United States to make sure we were in the right environment with was so crucial to giving us opportunities and mentors to provide us with the proper guidance!

My dad sold one business to enter another, it was his passion to fill a need in the art world, and to help others. He taught me, and now his wisdom lives on through me as I pass it along to you. We are never too old to follow our hearts, to try something new and to help others, and to become successful in our life.

It is my goal to empower you to find success, and it isn't always just about how much money you make. I was inspired by Steve Jobs, a man who understood this wisdom at the end of his life. He had the resources to buy anything he wanted, except happiness and health. Let's not miss this valuable lesson and learn from his mistakes.

A focus solely on making money does not empower you to have a happy life. Sure, we need money to be responsible and earn our way through life so we are not a burden on others. As we age, most of us are challenged by some health issues, but if we make our health a priority, we can manage our health with exercise and diet much better than having to depend on medication. Staying healthy is so important! At this time in my life, nearly 69 years of age, I am proud that I have chosen to make my health a priority. I am blessed and grateful that I am not dependent on medication to stay healthy as are so many my age. I have focused on being a loving partner to my husband, with respect and acceptance. With success, I can keep in touch with my loving sisters and brothers by being there if they need me, enjoying my dogs who, in return, love me unconditionally, and helping others live out the success they want in their life. These things have created happiness in me.

It is essential to decide what you value in your life, everything starts there. Then make your priorities in life in line with your values. It is your choice to live the way you want to live. You make decisions, right or wrong, and then don't blame others for them, you are responsible. I have learned the importance of taste, "The salt and the sweet of life," my parents would say. That's why I'm here, and that is why you are here reading this book and being in search of your best and most successful life.

CHAPTER 1

Our Parents - Our Heritage

"Adversity often activates a strength we did not know we had."
Joan Walsh Anglu

Our Heritage

Indonesia was my home for the first 18 years of my life. In grade school geography, I recall learning Indonesia is a country made up of 13,000 islands. I later learned, there are more than 13,000 islands. Some references show as many as 18,000 islands in Indonesia; this discrepancy is due to islands that disappear during high tide and reappear at low tide.

I was born in Indonesia, as were my parents, grandparents, and great grandparents. Even though I am the fourth generation to be born in Indonesia, I am not considered Indonesian because of our Chinese heritage. This is difficult to explain to my American friends because to claim to be Indonesian, no matter how many generations of your family are born in Indonesia, you are not considered Indonesian if you have a Chinese, European, or American heritage.

As a child, I was confused because some of my friends said I was Chinese. I wondered why I was not an Indonesian like them. I was born in Indonesia. It wasn't until it was explained to me that I understood. Unlike in the United States, if you are born in the United States, you are considered an American, no matter your family's origin. This is not the case in Indonesia. You are Indonesian only if your ancestry or lineage is Indonesian.

My paternal great-grandparents were born in Indonesia. They were born in the small town of Sungailiat on Bangka, an island southeast of Sumatra which is one of Indonesia's large islands. Their parents were also born in the same town. I was told they were very successful entrepreneurs. Both passed away at a very young age. The cause of their death was unknown, but it appeared to be unexpected. They left my grandfather and his sister with no one to care for them. There were no banks yet, I was told, their money, jewelry, and other valuable possessions were hidden and never found. The servants were able to sell the house, which was the only possession that the children had, and the money helped towards the care of the children at the orphanage where they were sent.

My paternal grandfather was born in Sungailiat on the island of Bangka in 1884. His name was Bong Min Djoen. My mom described him as a very kind, soft-spoken, and gentle person. He loved my mother and thought she was wonderful. My Mom cared for him because of his kindness and because he was easy to talk to, and she felt an obligation to do so. Because he grew up in an orphanage, he had no real father role model. Later on in life, I reflected on my paternal grandfather's journey. I never got a chance to know him. As a child, he did not have loving parents, this likely caused him to have less confidence as he became an adult. Through him, I learned having kids is much easier than being a parent. This may have been why he married my grandmother. As is the case in many families, our securities as well as our insecurities are passed down in our families.

This seemed to be something that my father worried about. Not only did my father grow up without a father's influence, but his father also did. My grandfather's father had died when he was young. These may have been contributing factors leading to his marriage to my grandmother. My paternal grandmother was controlling and ambitious.

Although my parents were of Chinese heritage, my siblings and I were not raised with tradition. My mom, a strong-minded woman, decided all her children would all be treated equally. My dad supported this idea. So in my family, the girls were valued and given opportunities just like my brothers.

When I grew up in Indonesia, there was no provision to care for the elderly such as social security or nursing homes. Families took care of their own unlike in the US today.

My paternal grandmother did not like my mom, even from the beginning. My grandmother invested her time in her boys, not girls. She believed they would care for her as she got older. My mom was an independent and intelligent woman, my grandmother may have felt threatened, or maybe she just didn't want to invest time and energy building a relationship with her. My grandmother valued grandsons more than granddaughters because she believed the girls would marry and move with their husbands. She had not nurtured a relationship with my father because she believed his older brothers would take on the responsibility to care for her as she aged. As I grew up, I don't remember many things about my father's mother. She never came to my home for visits because her expectation was for us to visit her in her own home. She was a widow and alone, my grandfather passed away at a young age, which happened before I was born.

My father's older brothers were given a lot of attention and were sent to school by my grandmother. They were spoiled, and they had difficulty making it in the real world as they became adults. Unlike my father, who needed to fend for himself, they never learned to be responsible. Of the four brothers, my father was the most successful. As it turned out, each of the other sons had large families and were never able to financially care for their parents as tradition dictated. Ironically, my father was the one who ended up taking care of her because he was the one that was financially able to do so.

My father cared for his mother until she passed away. He purchased a house for her because she wanted to live independently. She was proud of her home. I don't have good memories of her. When I was fourteen, she passed away. I didn't feel a loss like one might think a grandchild should feel, nor did my sisters.

My maternal grandparents were born in Sungailiat, like my father's parents, in Bangka, the late 1800s. My maternal grandfather, his name, Tjoeng Sin Fat, was born on January 25, 1898. My maternal Grandmother, Ng A Goan was born on October 9, 1902. We shared many things in common, like looking at both sides of issues, problems, or stories. It may be because we both share the same horoscope sign, Libra, which is a sign of balance. I have a birthmark just like hers. It is even in the same location on my body.

My maternal grandparents had respected my father for having kept his promise to them and taking such good care and providing for my mom. My grandmother spent a great deal of time with us, and she didn't care if we were girls or boys. She loved all of us, just the same. She spent lots of time being a wonderful grandmother to my siblings and me. She instilled in me the value of being a girl and was a role model to me. She showed my siblings and I what a wonderful grandmother could be and girls have the same rights as the boys in the family and shouldn't feel inferior because we were girls.

When she passed away at 63 years old, I was almost 15 and devastated, I felt the loss deeply. It seemed unfair to me, and I didn't understand why she had died when my other grandmother lived so much longer. She had been diagnosed with colon cancer twelve years earlier. My dad made sure she had the best medical care and surgeons. In those days, surgery was performed, and it left the patient with a "stoma" or pouch. It was an external bag which filled with waste material, and it needed to be drained often. My father cared for her after surgery in a loving way. Now that I have had time to think about it, she died too young. But back then, I thought she was very old.

Besides learning from our parents, my sisters and I learned equality from my maternal grandmother. She loved to cook for us. She would ask each of us what foods were our favorites, and she would make a point to make them when she could. If we didn't like the meal, she would always encourage us to try it anyway. She would tell us, "You never know if you might like it or not unless you try it." She was a disciplinarian because it is so important to have good behavior.

During the last years of her life, she never complained about cancer or her stoma. She made sure we understood life is about adjusting to your circumstances. Just because you have cancer and the doctor tells you that you don't have long to live, this doesn't mean you can't be happy to live out your days with what you do have. You must move on, don't complain, be positive, and make the best of your circumstances and what you have.

My grandfather was very handy with tools and spent a lot of time with my brother Wendel, teaching him how to fix things. My youngest brother was too little to learn to fix things. I recall my grandfather taught Wendel, how to take a door off the hinges. So Wendel decided to try it one day by himself. The door fell onto the floor, so he told everyone it fell by itself. But we all knew that he had done it. He loved emulating my grandfather. When our grandfather passed away, I was already in college and didn't have the budget to go home to Indonesia for his funeral.

Papi's Childhood

My Dad's name was, Bong Fo Djie, I call him Papi, his nickname was Eddy. As Papi told me, he was born on July 21, 1925. He was the eighth of 11 children and the second youngest son. Many women and their babies didn't survive childbirth, which was the case with two of his sisters. He was born in a small town, Pangkal Pinang, the capital of the Island of Bangka, a small island southeast of Sumatra, one of Indonesia's large islands.

Because they were older than my father, my father's brothers were given all the advantages that their family could afford. Typically, sons, especially the oldest son, receive education and opportunities more so than the younger sons and girls; this is because the expectation is they will care for their parents when they are to old to care for themselves.

Women were considered to be a minority at the time my father was born, and they had few rights afforded to them in Indonesia. Wives had nothing to say about the decisions in the family. Even now, traditional parents hope to have boys. The more boys in a family, the better because they need to have a backup plan to ensure someone could care for them as they age. The girls were not expected to care or provide for their aging parents.

Dad's parents were impoverished, and they didn't have the financial resources to invest in all of their children. At that time, my dad was age seven, and the youngest boy. His younger brother was not born yet. Unfortunately, dad's mom believed in a fortunetellers' guidance and took her four sons to see which ones would be the most successful. Because they were poor, she could only afford to educate three of the four boys.

The fortuneteller first chose the two smartest ones, and then she explained that my dad was the fourth likely to be successful and would not be able to take care of his parents in their later years. She said he wasn't as smart as his brothers. His mother believed the fortune teller's advice. He was sent away to work and support himself because they could no longer care for him.

Papi was on his own from the age of seven and went to live with a couple who owned a rubber plantation, a big industry starting in the early 1900s. The couple called him Eddy, and they saw him as very driven with a strong will to survive. He went to school, which was far from the plantation. He walked at least one hour each way he was so disciplined and determined to become educated. He didn't need much for his living expenses, so the owner, being a man of integrity, saved Eddy's extra money for him. His only activities were eating, sleeping, going to school, and then work. He had no social life until his teen years.

In early 1942, Indonesia was occupied by the Japanese. Later on in the same year, the Japanese took many strong Indonesian men to Burma's labor force camps. Eddy was seventeen at that time and considered an adult. He was a strong, healthy, and energetic young man. Eddy knew it just a matter of time until he would be sent to the camp. He also realized if that happened, he likely wouldn't return. The rumors were that the men in the camps were worked so hard and fed so little that few survived. He knew he needed to do something.

The Japanese were a proud people, and they wanted the Indonesian people to learn Japanese, not the reverse. Eddy, being wiser than his years, saw an opportunity when a Japanese officer noticed him because he was hardworking, obedient, and respectful. The officer enjoyed his curiosity, and Eddy took the opportunity to ask questions. By engaging with the officer, he learned the Japanese language. After some time, he asked the officer if he would help him become an interpreter. Eddy worked for him and was never sent to the labor camps in Burma.

Eddy learned quickly and mastered the language, and he became an interpreter to help the officer who had befriended him. Sometimes he would carefully interpret the words to protect the Indonesian people by changing the meaning just slightly to favor them, keeping them safe. The Japanese officer had no idea what he was doing.

One time Eddy was riding a bike and was in a hurry, and he didn't stop to bow to a Japanese soldier. The soldier told him to get off his bike and bow and carry his bike until he was told he could put it down. He was beaten and whipped.

Eddy spoke of this time in his life rarely, as he was beaten many times. Because of how they treated people, he despised the Japanese for what they did to the Indonesian people. Years later, he still had nightmares from the brutality he saw and experienced during this time in his life. He survived the war by choosing to learn and being proactive.

Throughout his life, Eddy was determined to prove the fortuneteller was wrong, he was a survivor.   At each juncture of his life he sought out somebody to help him accomplish his goals. He knew what it took to survive in the world, this is a quality that served him throughout his life. He taught me his wisdom and philosophies, how to stay focused on my goals and have discipline, no matter how long it takes and ever allow other people to dictate your future. This served him throughout his life and was an example for as a formula for success.

There was good that came from Eddy's experience during the war. His choice to learn another language gave him another opportunity he used to his advantage after the war. He thought outside the box. He was self-confident rather than being paralyzed by fear, as so many people were. He was respected for his abilities and talents, and because of his penchant to make the most of a difficult situation, he survived and later used what he learned to create success in his life.

Mami's Childhood

My Mom, Tjoeng Wie Lan, I call her Mami (Mommy). My Mami was born on January 30, 1925, on the same island as my father, Bangka, but in a different city, Sungailiat. She came from a "well to do" family and was the only girl. She had three older brothers and two younger brothers.

Mami told me two stories from her childhood. The first one caused her to have a fear of dogs. When she was a child, she was bitten by a dog who had rabies. In Indonesia, the only treatment available for rabies was to receive many injections to prevent the rabies infection from taking hold in the body. If that were to have happened, she would have died. Because her family had the means to pay for the costly treatment, her life was spared. Having money didn't help with the pain involved or keep her from the emotional scars. She remembered it being a very painful experience and from then on she connected it with all dogs.

The second story happened during the time when the Japanese invaded Indonesia. Like my Dad, she didn't like the Japanese soldiers, but for a different reason. During the war, food was expensive, and any meat was incredibly hard to find. Pork was considered a delicacy, and few could afford it. One day the Japanese soldiers came to her home and took her beloved pet pig to eat. She was devastated, it hurt her so deeply, and she grieved for many years. Because of the memory of this loss, she wouldn't eat Pork for many years.

Mami finished high school, which was very unusual at that time for anyone but especially for a woman. Her parents wanted her to be an educated wife one day, so they gave her all of the opportunities to learn the skills she would need to run a household of her own. For them, this did not include college, as we might think for today's women.

In these times, a college education was not considered more important than cooking, sewing, and caring for a family. For her, it was another type of education that includes specialized skills such as learning to be a chef, a pastry chef, and a seamstress. She was serious about all of these skills and was preparing herself through these courses to be the best wife for her future husband. She earned many certificates for specialties; all were geared towards what her parents thought would help them present their daughter as a good wife to a successful man. This was very important to Mami's parents as they believed these qualifications were necessary for them to present her to an eligible man who would be worthy of their daughter.

During this time, it was the custom, especially the women born to wealthy families, for the parents to choose their daughters' spouses. Mami's parents were planning to choose her husband from successful men in the community, but Mami had other ideas. She was very determined, independent, and very intelligent. She wanted to choose her own husband and not have one selected for her.

Wie and Eddy Meet

There was only one problem, Mami didn't love any of the wealthy men that were available. She fell in love with a teacher. At that time, being a teacher was not a noble career, at least in her parent's eyes. A doctor, engineer, or successful businessman were considered noble vocations. Her parents adamantly opposed the marriage. They even paid the man to leave their city and not contact her again. He took the money and left town as instructed. Mami was broken-hearted because she never heard from him again. It took her a long time for her to have an interest in dating anyone.

Then Wie (Mami) met dad, Eddy. He was very charming, good looking, and caring. She fell in love with him for his drive, along with all of his other positive qualities. Many women liked him for his charm. She noticed he could talk to anyone, and she liked that quality. Wie was determined to marry him. However, Eddy had only completed high school and couldn't afford a college education, and the Japanese had invaded Indonesia, forcing him to give up pursuing further education. To support himself, he had to join the workforce.

Wie didn't care that he was not college-educated, she loved his determination and ambitious nature, and she admired his intelligence.

Eddy loved all of the qualities he found in Wie. She was beautiful and educated in the ways that culture dictated. He felt very fortunate that Wie fell in love with him. Her position in society was not what he was attracted to. However, he did realize it made Wie who she was. He was poor, and he wasn't the man her parents would likely approve. She could have any man. This caused him to be grateful that she wanted to marry him. They were both determined to marry despite her parents' opposition. Her parents were adamantly against the relationship, and as they had done before, offered him a bribe to leave Wie. They would have paid him to go far away and never contact her again. However like many age-old romantic stories, Wie had different ideas, they were in love, and Eddy was determined to marry her.

Wie's parents had invested in her. This was very important because if the wife needed to work in their culture, it was shameful and a bad reflection on her family. Only a successful man could give her the kind of life they expected of him. It wasn't only Wie's life that would be affected if she didn't marry the right person. The children would suffer if they couldn't afford an education. This is highly valued in the Chinese family. The family had a great deal of pressure on them because otherwise, it would cause shame to the extended family. If you think about it, this way of thinking is honorable, as the parents were very concerned about their daughter's well being. More than that, they wanted to ensure their grandchildren would be cared for and would be educated. Their daughter's husband needed to be a good provider, so their daughter would stay home to run the household.

When Eddy didn't accept their bribe, they respected him, and after discovering how serious they were, they got to know him more and saw qualities in him that they liked. Still, they were afraid of her future, and that he may not give Wie the life she was born and groomed to live. But they were starting to see they were not winning the battle of being able to choose her husband. Wie considered running away with Eddy, but she loved her parents and did not want hurt them. Eddy wanted to do the honorable thing and ask her parents for her hand in marriage. So, although it wasn't easy, Wie's parents eventually conceded and gave their approval to allow them to marry because they saw the determination in both of them. Eddy promised Wie and her parents that she would be an honored wife and would not need to ever work to support the family.

Eddy's parents were not involved in the decision of marriage as he had been independent of them since early childhood. And so, Eddie and Wie married, on March 6, 1949, in Bandung, where they met at age 24. Eddy delivered on his promise to Wie's parents and gave her a life they wanted her to have. His commitment had been heartfelt and was as important to him as it was for them. Wie never had to work to support the family throughout their 54 years of marriage. My mother and father worked together, which was her choice, as partners managing the art gallery after my youngest brother started the 3rd grade.

Wie and Eddy's Early Life

Shortly after my parents married, they moved to Jakarta. During the Dutch colonization of Indonesia, Bandung was considered a prosperous city. The Dutch considered moving the capital of West Java to Bandung because of its strategic location. Jakarta (formerly known as Batavia) was the capital of West Java province. Because the Japanese invaded Indonesia in early 1942, the plan was never materialized. Many Chinese descendants who lived on the island of Bangka moved to Bandung to have a better life. My maternal grandparents and their unmarried children (including my mom) moved to Bandung because the city was very prosperous. They opened a restaurant that served Chinese with Dutch-influenced foods. Later the restaurant became known as one of the best Chinese-Dutch restaurants in Bandung. Both my grandmother and Wie were the chefs at the restaurant. Wie was also known as the Pastry Chef, who made many of the customers' favorite Dutch pastries. She also held her own cooking classes. Eddy had initially gone to Bandung because the city was very prosperous. He wanted to find a better job and have the opportunity to have a better life. Bandung had a good community of Chinese people similar to the many communities we see in large cities in the United States today, often called "China Town." Bandung became the capital of West Java after Indonesia declared its independence in 1945 when Jakarta became its capital.

Shortly after they were married, my parents went to Jakarta and registered on August 9, 1949, to receive a marriage certificate and to get promotional gifts for newlyweds. It was also because Jakarta had become the capital of Indonesia. Both Eddy and Wie were born the same year, but mom lied about her birth date because she didn't want people to know that she was older than her husband. During that time, it was not acceptable to marry an older woman. Wie told everyone she was almost one year younger than Eddy, but she was actually a few months older than him.

At the beginning of their marriage, they struggled financially. Eddy worked two jobs to afford the rented home where they lived. Although Wie worked as a pastry chef teacher and seamstress before they married, she didn't work after they married. This would have disgraced the family, and Eddy didn't want to break the promise he had made to Wie and her parents.

Life Lessons: your reflection

A thought to inspire you:

"I can be changed by what happens to me. But I refuse to be reduced by it."
Maya Angelou

What does this mean in your life? ....

....

....

....

Questions to empower you:

What valuable lessons have you learned from your family relationships? ....

....

....

....

Who made investments in your life, and how do you express gratitude to
them? ....

....

....

....

How have you adjusted for circumstances you can't control? ....

....

....

....

Have you known anyone who has faced difficult situations and handled them with dignity and strength? How did it help you see difficult situations differently? ....

....

....

Reflections: what will you apply in your life? ....

....

....

....

....

....

....

....

....

....

....

....

"You are in charge of your future,
don't allow other people to dictate your future."

Angeline Benjamin

CHAPTER 2

My Childhood in Indonesia

"The best way to raise positive children in a negative world
is to have positive parents who love them unconditionally
and serve as excellent role models"
Zig Ziglar

My Early Childhood

My birth name was Bong Mei Lie. I was born on October 13, 1951. I am the firstborn child in my family. Mami delivered me past the due date the doctor had given her. Because I was born near midnight, my family teased me about being a night person. Today, my name is Angeline Liestyawati Benjamin, legally changed from Bong Mei Lie.

During the 50's it was common for the fathers not to be in the delivery room. So my father was not present at my birth. He was glad about this because he couldn't bear seeing Wie in pain, nor was he good around blood. After I was born, the doctor told him he had a beautiful baby girl, but later, he was puzzled when he saw me. He disagreed with the doctor because I looked wrinkled and was not what he had anticipated. He also thought I was sad because I was so quiet and didn't cry or smile.

Papi had only seen pictures of older babies, not newborn babies. He didn't realize all babies looked wrinkled at first. He thought the best thing to do was to name me Mei Lie, which means beautiful in Chinese. With this as my name, everyone would be calling me beautiful, so I would believe this was true.

When people tell me they think I am a serious person, I can confidently say, yes, my natural tendencies are to be a focused person with intention and achievement in mind. This was evident even from birth. I realized and accepted this about myself after taking many personality assessments, all reflecting similar results. This is a part of my DNA, and I am proud of who I am and how I turned out because of all the support I received throughout my life's journey.

As our parents had done with me, they tended to name their kids based on their first impression. I later discovered this is similar to Native American traditions of naming their children after something that happens right after birth. My sister, Indria, was screaming at the top of her lungs and had lots of energy, so they named her Mei Ling, which means dragon. My sister, born after Indria looked fragile and delicate, so they named her "flower," or Mei Hwa. My youngest sister's name is Mei Chen because she had her eyes wide open when she was born, so they thought she was a "Pearl."

My parents told me I was a happy baby, a joyful baby. This may be because I was the first baby, or maybe it is because of my personality, but I rarely cried and was content to be in a crib or play area, and I loved music. Even when my diaper needed to be changed, it didn't bother me. I would laugh often, and almost anyone could make me laugh, so people liked being around me. I would go to anyone, even strangers, and they said, I loved it when people talked to me. Because of this, my parents were very protective, as are most first-time parents.

My siblings and I loved playing together, and we rarely got into arguments like I hear kids today. Because I was the oldest, they always listened to me. When we played, if I wanted to be a mom or a dad, they would agree. Then I would tell them what they were going to be in our make-believe game. We never experienced bullying. I think it was because we were always together, even when we went to school. No one ever tried to take advantage of us or harm us. There is strength in numbers and my sisters and I always stuck together.

My parents told me I was very independent, determined, and silently stubborn as a child. When I wanted something, I didn't give up until I got it. When I tried something new, I wouldn't give up until I did it. When I struggled with it, I would not let my parents know, and I didn't want any help. I would say, "Just give me some time to figure it out."

I did not like to climb trees like my sister Indria did. So I asked Indria to help me learn how so I could get comfortable and confident. I did not want my parents to know. I guess I was a very cautious girl, and I was too proud to tell my parents I was afraid. I would never say to my parents that I couldn't do something. That wasn't how I operated. I wanted to do it my way.

Indria was a tom-boy and was the one no one wanted to mess with. She protected her siblings from anyone who might want to do harm to us. I believe people are bullies because they lack confidence or are insecure. Parents can help their children by building their self-worth and confidence, yet also teaching them about kindness. If they reinforce that their kids are smart, strong, and empower them to try things and find what they are good at, this will help them not take it out on others. This is what our parents did with us. If I did something that wasn't what they would expect from me, they would just let me know that they expected more of me and that they trusted me to make better decisions in the future. I wasn't resentful, but I did want to try harder the next time. Being the oldest, I was responsible for setting the example and felt proud to have this responsibility.

Also, if I wanted something that I was not sure my parents would let me have, I would ask strategically. I would never go to my parents demanding to have something. Papi would always ask us, "How bad do you want it." My father and I had the same kind of drive. So I knew if I wanted something, all I needed to do was work for it. My strategy was to be good first. One time I remember wanting a Vespa called a Lambretta, it would help us get around, but it wasn't as fast or dangerous as a motorcycle. Indria was more adventurous than me, so I told her about my idea. I knew she would agree because it was a good idea. Of course, she loved it! So we developed our strategy, how should we approach our parents to buy one for us? I thought that if we told them that we would get excellent grades in all of the important subjects the school emphasized, like math and science, etc., they might agree to get one.

My parents didn't really think we would be able to achieve our lofty goals. And of course, they supported us in getting the best grades. They didn't realize my sister and I were very determined to get the Vespa, we were able to achieve the excellent grades we promised at the end of the school year. Papi and Mami, especially Mami, didn't like the idea of us riding a Vespa around town. Because Papi felt they needed to honor their promise, in the end we got the Vespa!

My Early School Years

In Indonesia, the school started with pre-kindergarten at about five years of age, which is when I started. It was mostly to get the new students comfortable being in a school setting and socializing with other kids. We spent the day singing and playing. I refused to go to school unless Indria, my sister, could go with me. So my parents asked the principal and the teacher if my sister could start school with me, even though she was a year and three months younger. They told the teacher I was shy and uncomfortable and would be happier with my sister came with me. At that time, I was nearly five, and my parents didn't want me to wait another year when Indria was old enough to attend school. I suspect my parents had some influence on the school's approval.

One more factor to my parents requesting my sister attend school at the same time as me, was when Josie was born, my mom needed to pay extra attention to her because she was sickly. When my fourth sister and then later my brothers came along, my mom was glad that we were in school together.

The teacher thought she would try letting my sister join me at school, as long as Indria did not disturb the class or be destructive. What ended up happening was Indria was happy and enjoyed being in class with me, and I was happy to be with her. She was very capable of sitting quietly when she needed to be, and she would raise her hand to speak as instructed. So the teacher let her stay in class.

Even today, my sister and I are very close. Maybe because of our ages, or our shared experiences, and also being great playmates as children. We both loved learning, and because we were in the same classes, we did our homework together. Indria was good in math and helped me, and I was more verbal and good in science, so I helped her.

I always felt like it was a privilege to have gone to a private school. My dad worked hard as an entrepreneur to provide a good education that offered us the best private schools in Indonesia. The school we first attended was a Catholic school, called Regina Pacis. Because my parents learned that catholic schools were one of the best private schools in Indonesia, and they wanted to be a part of the Catholic community through our school. Religious education was something they believed in. Our whole family became Catholic and were baptized into the Catholic faith and devoted followers and active Catholic church members. Dad did many things to benefit the church and was very respected.

There was an entrance exam in first grade to ensure your success in the private schools, they were open to anyone who could afford it and who could pass the entrance exam. In public schools, there was no entrance exam, and they were less expensive than private schools. The expectation was also that you stay focused on your schooling. It was a no-nonsense school, and if you caused any problems, you would be kicked out. My parents made sure we understood this.

The Chinese Indonesian was a course taught in my elementary school to the children, and was one of my first experiences in early school. Many thought at the time it was a great advantage for the students. Bahasa Indonesian is the primary and official language of Indonesia. However, there are over 300 different native languages spoken throughout the country. All courses are taught in the Indonesian language. Indonesian speaking and writing were primary courses, and we had to have a passing grade to go to the next at the end of each school year. Other languages taught were German, English, and the Chinese language were the optional courses we could take. We were considered a citizen of China because of our heritage, not our birth, so having Chinese taught in school was a concern to my parents because of the political and social implications.

At that time, it had become apparent to Papi we needed further protection, even though it had not gotten too bad yet. Papi was a proactive thinker, especially when it came to the safety of his family! So we changed schools and attended another Catholic school, Tarakanita II. This school was attended by both Chinese and Indonesian students. The education they provided was superior to the other schools, and our parents felt it would be less likely that we would be discriminated against. The kids that attended this school needed to have the means and political stature to be accepted. It was where you could get the best education. Wealthy families did not send their kids to public schools. My parents did not allow us to learn the Chinese language to further prove our loyalty to Indonesia. Both my parents spoke Chinese but didn't teach us.

To protect us even further, my dad, well-known in our community as a successful entrepreneur and natural leader, was voted into a school board position. He later became the president of the school board. He did this because his strategy was always to ensure the safety of our family.

Although I did very well in math, it didn't come easy to me. I studied very hard, and Indria helped me. After school, I came home and did my homework right away. I was very disciplined and focused even at an early age. I helped model self discipline for my sister Indria, and for my younger siblings.

In fifth grade, while at Tarakanita II, I noticed the other kids listened to me, and my teachers said I was an influencer. They voted me to be the president of the class. There was no campaign; that would be looked at as being boastful, and humility was valued. Peers vote after one or more candidates were nominated, and then there was a winner.

Because I was the president of the class, there were advantages and responsibilities. I had to set a good example, and I couldn't get into any trouble. I also wanted to make sure my sister stayed out of trouble because it would reflect on our family and me. I was not interested in being fashionable. It was more important that I get good grades, and I set an example as a leader. Being popular was not my objective. This wasn't important, except to be the best example I could be.

In Catholic school, discipline is a big deal. We have all heard the stories of the strict nuns who used physical punishment with rulers on the knuckles and pulling ears. I witnessed this. Some of the infractions could be having dirty fingernails that were checked by the teachers. If you didn't pass inspection, the nuns might hit your knuckles with a ruler.

My dad didn't believe in this, because in the war he was beaten by the Japanese officers, he didn't want the children to be subjected to physical harm. He felt physical harm didn't help kids be better people. He felt the removal of privileges or making them complete undesirable tasks was much more effective. He believed you could have the kids stay after school, or write a reinforcing message on the blackboard, like, "I will not do (whatever they did)," 100 times or more on the blackboard. Or they have to clean the bathroom as their punishment. Some type of chore was given, something they didn't like to do, like sweeping the classroom floor. He believed in making a difference in the lives of kids. An expected consequence of bad behavior would be doing something to make amends. These things were a deterrent to the kids acting up at school and more effective. Also, they believed if you bullied someone at school, it deserved severe punishment. So he proposed a change in the policy. It was widely accepted and physical punishment was made no longer acceptable.

Every quarter they issued a report card, and parents had to sign the report card. In each grade, you were given a final exam. Anything that was not a passing score was marked in red. The grades were from one to ten, with ten being perfect. They never gave a ten because, in their minds, no student was perfect. The highest grade was nine, and that was very rare. My grades were mostly sevens and eights, or maybe one or two nines, in science, of course. It was rare for me to get a nine! My sister Indria received mostly eights and nines, especially in math, she always got a nine.

If you couldn't pass the grade, you then had to stay in the same grade for another whole year. Most kids were really embarrassed when this happened, and often they even went to another school because of the shame they felt. A few would repeat the grade again and didn't seem to care at all.

Even when I didn't get the highest grades, I was proud that I was a leader. This was very important to me. I didn't get good grades in art, drawing, music, or cursive writing skills. My Indonesian writing skills were average. Fortunately, as long as these grades were above 5, it was considered acceptable, because they were not essential subjects and not needed to be moved to the next grade. The most important subjects were math and science, civics, Indonesian language, history, social science, and religion, you must pass these, and I always did and achieved above-average grades.

In the sixth grade in Indonesia, it was the last grade before junior high school. A final exam was always required before one could move on to the next grade, but it was a more detailed and difficult exam at the end of sixth grade. It covered all of the learning principles from first to sixth grade. You must pass this exam to go to junior high school.

I studied very hard, my parents told me I didn't want to do anything else for months. I was so determined. After school, I would study. I wanted to get the highest grade possible. When we got the results, my sister Indria got a perfect score in math. I did very well, but not perfect. I was so mad at myself, so disappointed, I silently cried. I asked myself, "Why couldn't I get a perfect score in math? I studied so hard." I received an eight in math and eights and nines in the other subjects.

I was very hard on myself, but now I realize that each of us has different talents. I am determined and ambitious, and a good leader and I did my best, even then. I remember being so proud of myself that passed the difficult exam the first time I took it, I could go on to junior high school. My hard work paid off!

No one in my family failed to go on to the next grade. It was not an option for us to fail! A good education was important to my parents. We even had tutors in fifth and sixth grades. This was not because we got bad grades, but because our parents wanted us to have the best education. Our teacher was our tutor, and she got paid extra for tutoring Indria and me.

I really enjoyed the tutoring sessions at our teacher's home. She let us come early to have fruit from her trees and to have it before she helped us with our homework. My sister loved climbing her trees to pick it for us.

Our teacher and tutor's name was Bu Bambang. In the Indonesian language, Bu is a greeting to an older woman giving respect, and Bambang was her last name. As I recall, all our female teachers were called "Bu" and then their name. Bu Bambang had a reputation for being strict, and some of the kids didn't like her. I really liked her, and I would sit in the front of the class. She would remind me of my responsibilities but I was never resentful of her correction because deep down, I knew she meant well.

I tended to take responsibility for my siblings. Being the oldest child, I felt it was my responsibility to keep them safe. To me, it was a privilege, not a disadvantage. I guess even at a young age, I liked to be in charge. Sometimes my sibling would call me bossy. I call it knowing what I want and being determined to go for it.

Indonesian Political Climate

When I was a young child, I was not aware of the discrimination against the Chinese in Indonesia. I didn't suffer from discrimination, mainly because my parents protected my siblings and me. This was very important to my parents because there was political unrest in Indonesia at that time, and the Chinese were targeted as possible communists. The people who governed Indonesia feared communism. In the late evening of September 30 of 1965, a group of Indonesian military personnel captured and murdered six powerful generals. This coupled with the fall of President Sukarno, Indonesia's first president. It began about one year of the great rebellion. This is referred to in history as the Indonesian Communist Purge. From what I remember, it involved a group that supported the Indonesian Communist Party. At that time, the army leadership insisted it was a plot to seize power from the Indonesian government, which was not communist. In the months that followed, the military slaughtered hundreds of thousands of people, all were communists or alleged communists. According to Wikipedia, there could have been up to three million people that may have been killed during this mass genocide. My father was wise to protect us, and do everything to keep us safe. He never spoke of this to us because they did not want to pass to us any fear or negative thoughts about our heritage.

During this year of rebellion, there were months we could not attend school because the hatred put us at risk. Even years afterward, there were many demonstrations throughout Indonesia, including at my school.

To further protect us and keep us from discrimination, and from being accused of supporting the communist party, Papi went to the court system and provided a written declaration to Indonesia's government. This declaration confirmed that we all were born in Indonesia, and we chose to release or give up our Chinese citizenship. Many Chinese dependents did this during this period of unrest in Indonesian history. This was documented officially in the courts on December 28, 1960. On August 1, 1967, our Chinese names were legally removed, and we adopted Christian - Indonesian names. Papi impressed upon me the importance of these documents, and I have kept them safe all of my life. The decision to change our names removed a part of our Chinese identity.

My name became Angeline Liestyawati Benjamin instead of Bong Mei Lie. My dad chose Benjamin as our last name because it was his Christian baptismal name. Angeline was my baptismal name, Liestyawati is my Indonesian legal name, and Benjamin became my last name. The Indonesian people at that time had only one name typically. It serves as their full name with no first or last name. My Indonesian name is Liestyawati, which I still use as my middle name.

Our new names were acceptable during the unrest and much safer because it showed the officials that we are not communist. We were now identified by our Indonesian names rather than Chinese names, so we wouldn't be associated with the Chinese Communist Party. Although my dad went to great extents to protect us, one thing couldn't be changed. That was our Chinese appearance. Because of this, we still experienced the discrimination that my parents feared would keep us from attending the university of our choice.

As Chinese-Indonesians, we didn't have all of the rights of those who were Indonesian. My mom was charged more at the local market because she was Chinese. As a teenager, I saw this, and it made me angry. However, my mom didn't say anything. When I questioned her, she made sure I didn't say anything that could cause a scene. My parents taught us not to attract attention or to get in any trouble, at school, or in these situations. They taught us never to fight with someone who was Indonesian because it would almost automatically be our fault.

This didn't happen in stores owned by the Chinese, or larger stores. It was a common practice to have corruption, harassment, and discrimination towards Chinese people. If a Chinese business person had a silent business partner who was Indonesian, they were not harassed because the Chinese business owners paid a portion of the Indonesian partner's profit. A common practice to receive any preferential treatment was to pay money for the protection. This made my sister and I upset, and I would question it.

Without an Indonesian partner, there was no protection for the business. My parents saw this way of life and wanted to have a better life for our family. It took about one year of planning for things to fall in place. We were not allowed to discuss the plans with anyone. The only thing we could say to our friends was that my parents wanted us to study abroad to learn English, and after we finished college, we would be back in Indonesia.

I wanted to become a medical doctor. There were two types of medical schools in Indonesia: a public university or a private university. The University of Indonesia (a public university) made it very difficult for Chinese students to attend. Those who were Indonesians could get into the school much easier. And when they graduated, they received an internship right away and could begin practicing. This was not the case with Chinese descendants, who were rarely accepted, and had to wait many years to get an internship. The Chinese have a better chance of being accepted into private medical universities. However, when they graduate from medical school, they have to wait many years to do their internship and practice as a medical doctor. Because the University of Indonesia medical school has to approve your medical degree. It could take as many as five years before getting a medical degree, which was needed before starting an internship. And the internships were usually in undesirable areas. This was to deter them from trying, or in some cases, a monetary bribe might allow a student to receive preferred treatment.

My youngest sister Bernadette was in the top 5% of her class and wanted to become a doctor as well. Her best chance for her to get a medical degree without waiting so many years was to go to a public medical school. The best public medical school in Indonesia is The University of Indonesia. She did not get accepted at the University of Indonesia because she is Chinese. A part of the application was to attach a photo. What discouraged my parents and my sister was when she found out one of her Indonesian friends, a below-average student graduating from high school, got into the University of Indonesia. Because of discrimination, my parents wanted to find a better way for my sister to get a good education. So they sent Bernadette to the United States. She had help from my sister Indria and her husband. So she started at a junior college in South Seattle, which allowed her to improve her English and make friends. Later on, she was accepted at the University of Washington. Bernadette was good at math like my sister Indria, including calculus. So she switched her major to applied math, which is now Biostatistics.

Dad A Successful Entrepreneur

Dad was an entrepreneur. As a child, we would visit Papi at work anytime we wanted. He was the boss and always made time for us.

In Jakarta, by the early 50s, movies were starting to become popular as an entertainment pastime. There were very few Indonesian movies, as no capital resources were going into the filming industry. Indonesian films were not well attended. People were going to the theaters to watch movies from the United States, Great Britain, India, and mostly Europe. However, they didn't entirely understand them because there were no subtitles at that time. Eddy realized a problem and quickly acted on his instincts to provide a solution, subtitles, which was his good fortune. This is how his company was born.

The name of his company was Insula. They translated all of the movies without any computerized assistance or software like today. Each film was carefully translated into Indonesian by people, and the subtitles were added at the bottom of the screen like they are today. As you can imagine, this was a huge deal. Most people who could afford to buy a movie ticket were able to read. Insula was an immediate success because of the high demand.

Another exciting part of our childhood was that our family got the first viewing of newly released children's movies before they were in the theater. I have many fond memories of our birthday parties. It was special because we invited kids from our school. Dad's business had a theater in it for movie viewings. These times were very memorable. The day after our parties, the kids who attended talked about how much fun we all had. I remember getting to see Snow White and the Seven Dwarfs, Sleeping Beauty, and Donald Duck, to name a few. Like many parents today, our parents were very selective in the movies we could watch.

Dad took into consideration the advantage he was given to be able to receive the movies in advance. He didn't want anyone to view him as taking advantage of the movie companies. At that time, because it was so new, no laws prevented the viewings as there is today.

My dad was self-taught and had a knack for learning languages. He learned to read and write in Indonesian as a child and later learned English, Dutch, Chinese, and Japanese during the war. He needed to write and speak in these languages to discuss the business with the movie companies and translate the movies. He met many interesting people as well as famous movie producers and stars in the entertainment industry.

We were treated very well by these people. Although our parents were very protective, we were allowed to socialize with many influential people. It was during these times we especially felt a sense a pride knowing that Papi was very successful. Papi being a successful entrepreneur didn't keep him from spending time with us. Mami was home and very supportive of him and each of us. We went on family vacations together, stayed at beautiful resorts. We had so much fun as a family.

We enjoyed the benefits of my dad's hard work, his connections in the movie industry, and the success he had. As the business became more successful, we moved to a nicer neighborhood, in a large house with five bedrooms. Each of the rooms in the house was very spacious. Papi sacrificed in his early years so we could have a childhood that gave us privilege and comforts. Although my parents could afford to buy us fancy clothes, toys, etc., we were raised to value money. Like most parents tell their kids, our parents told us money does not grow on trees. We were raised with that philosophy. However, It was shameful for us to work for money as teenagers, so we didn't have jobs. Later in my life, we found out that this was another one of my dad's promises to my grandparents. We received presents on our birthday and Christmas or when we did well in school. Because our parents did not spend money on us unnecessarily, we learned the value of earning things we wanted by being good, well-behaved students. Because my parents valued education and healthy lives, they spent money to send us to get an excellent education. We always have good quality foods, and we were never hungry! These values were passed down to my siblings and me, as our heritage is a beautiful gift.

My dad sold the movie subtitle business and followed his true passion, and with an idea to help artists, he opened an art gallery. He was very good at business leadership and interpersonal skills. Through my dad and being in the United States, I learned that one of the best skills to have is communication. My dad had natural communication skills, but he also had the admirable ability to create something out of what seemed to be nothing. He would get a vision of something the people needed and look for the solution. His businesses were successful because of his ability to have foresight into what problem needed a solution. He would find a way to make it a successful business.

His passion was art, and he loved painting. Eddy was admired for his innovative, big picture thinking. This was true for Insula, the subtitling business, and also in his art gallery. Like in the movie subtitle company, he saw a way to fill a need and profit from helping people. He did this while doing what he loved.

Most talented artists in Indonesia, even the well-known ones, didn't have a lot of money, and they used inexpensive and inferior quality materials. The clients that could afford the art wanted art made with better materials. So Eddy negotiated with the artists providing them with better quality materials. He promoted their work by having a showcase for them at the gallery to get higher-paying clients. In exchange for this, they would pay Eddy a portion of their profits. This made his business profitable, and he helped the starving artists. I learned later in my life that Eddy was admired because of his ability to see how to help others, and in doing so, it also helped his own efforts. His gallery became very well known nationally. Again his communication skills paid off because he was very good at telling stories about the artwork, paintings and woodwork statues, bone statues, and many types of multimedia pieces. He told stories about the artwork and also about the artists. People were interested in his vast knowledge of the materials used and how he acquired the works of art. Dad traveled throughout Java Island and Bali, looking for artists with talent. He had many teachers or what we would call mentors. He looked for older men to teach him what he needed to know. The Chinese highly respect their elders because they have experienced what we call "The salt of life." No matter what he needed to know, he found people who could teach him. He read books and studied artists from Europe like Vincent Van Gogh, Rembrandt Van Rijn, Pablo Picasso, Leonardo Da Vinci, Claude Monet, and more.

He conducted business for the art gallery, and by promoting many Indonesian artists, he never needed protection and wasn't harassed. He never paid bribes for safety that I was aware of, I believe it would have gone against his principles. Many of his customers were foreign diplomats, and people were in the entertainment industry. Also, some of the high ranking public officials and tourists were his customers.

I learned from Papi, if you want to survive discrimination or other challenges you may face, you need to be diligent and work smarter. You always have to have something to contribute. It might be called common sense or business strategies. The bottom line was Eddy felt he didn't want to be taken advantage of, nor did he take advantage of others. He always operated with good ethics and integrity because he told us otherwise, it would end badly.

Life Lessons: your reflection

A thought to inspire you:

"The goal of early childhood education should be to activate the child's natural desire to learn." Dr. Maria Montessori

What does this mean in your life? ....

....

....

Questions to empower you:

What valuable lessons have you learned from your childhood? ....

....

....

....

What childhood challenges helped form who you are today? ....

....

....

How can you work smarter in your life? ....

....

....

Do you have a solution to problems others may be facing? ....

....

....

Reflections: what will you apply in your life? ....

....

....

....

....

....

....

....

....

....

....

....

....

....

....

"As long as you have the passion, faith and are willing to work hard, you can do anything you want in this life."

Angeline Benjamin

CHAPTER 3

Coming To America

"Intellectual life requires for its expansion and manifestation the influences and assimilation of the interests and affections of others."
Jane Addams

My sister Indria and I arrived in the USA on January 6, 1970. This was the first time we had traveled overseas. We stopped in Hong Kong to get another suitcase, sweaters, and coats in preparation to live in California. The climate in California was different from at our home in Indonesia, to us it was going to be freezing cold.

When we arrived at LAX, the airport in Los Angeles, we were met by two nuns from Marywood High School. The Vice Principal and another nun welcomed us. There was a problem, the embassy in Indonesia had made a mistake, they forgot to give back the X-Ray films to prove that we had been cleared of Tuberculosis and able to travel in the United States. The Vice Principal took charge of the situation, explaining her position and we had been accepted as foreign students for Marywood High School with a student visa. She convinced the immigration officer to let us go to San Pedro for our clearance and she would take responsibility for us. They drove us to the Department of Public Health where we had another X-Ray and received the clearance we needed.

We learned from our parents before we left for this big adventure, it was very important that we assimilate into the American culture and the ways of life in the United States. Not only did they want us to adopt our new culture, but also be proud of our heritage, and not to expect it to be the other way around. They wanted us to understand that we were a guest in the country and we must be polite and kind.

While we were waiting for the results of the x-rays, we ate lunch. Because we had been taught by our parents to be polite, we didn't want to be rude and tell the nuns we were starving! One more problem, we could not understand them, because we thought they spoke too fast. We were so nervous, we could not say much and nor could we order the foods from the menu. So the nun's ordered sandwiches for us. The sandwich they gave us tasted really strange, not only were they foreign, but the beef tasted different to us because we did not eat cold cut meats. They ordered apple pie for dessert, explaining to us it was a very famous dessert in the U.S. so we were excited to try it. We didn't like the filling, we only liked the crust. They told us the filling was the best part, but we didn't think so.

After our lunch, the officials came to tell us that we had been cleared. By the time we got to the dormitory at our new school, it was late in the evening and we had fallen asleep in the car. It had been a long day. We didn't know it, but the students in the dorm had been waiting for our arrival. The nuns had made an exception and let the girls stay up later than usual so they could welcome us. We were the first Indonesian students to come to their school and live in the dormitory. They had done research in National Geographic Magazine, to find out what Indonesian people look like. The funny part was they saw the pictures of the native Indonesian dressed in a Sarong and Kebaya, and we didn't look like what they had expected.

Of course, we were not dressed in traditional clothing, we were wearing a pantsuit. Our parents wanted us to be prepared for the colder weather, so they had the seamstress make several pantsuits for us. At school we would wear a uniform, however, we wore our pantsuits when we were not in school. What we didn't know, the students were not allowed to wear pants. In the early '70s, pants were considered unladylike, so we were required to wear dresses or skirts. The nuns didn't say anything at first but later explained the required dress code.

The required uniform was a dress, so we wore long socks to the knee and Hush Puppy shoes. We were cold so we still wore our pants when we were not in school. We were not allowed to wear our uniform after school. We didn't know pants were against the rules. Some of the students living in the dormitory complained so the nuns changed the rule. After that, all of the students living in the dormitory were then allowed to wear pants when they were not in school. The students were so excited, they gave us the credit for the change, and thanked us.

At eighteen, being the oldest, I was responsible for the budget. We lived very frugally, everything was very expensive and we didn't want to waste our parent's money.

Because we were not able to speak or write in English, our focus was to learn English. Every afternoon after our regular classes we attended an accelerated English class for foreign students. While other students were enjoying the dormitory life of gathering to watch TV, we were learning to speak English in the language lab. We asked the teacher, one of the nun's to help us improve as fast as possible because we were very serious students. With her assistance, and our dedication our grades improved.

When we started in our American high school, it was mid-year and the beginning of the second semester. The school advisor told us were going to start as juniors, even though we would have been starting our senior year if we had stayed in Indonesia. This was because we had a language barrier to overcome, and we needed to complete all the required classes before we could graduate. If we had started during our senior year, it would have not given us enough time to learn English and study to pass the college entrance exams. We didn't mind this decision, in fact, we were relieved.

School in the United States was not what we experienced. In Indonesia, school starts in January, and you are promoted to the next grade level at that time. Another interesting difference between Indonesia and the US schools; Indonesian students stay in one classroom for all their subjects and the teachers move from class to class to teach their subjects. In the US, it is the opposite, the kids move from class to class while the teachers stay in one classroom. Also, in Indonesia, there was no "homeroom" period as it was in our new high school. In Indonesia, we had no lunch break, so our lunches were eaten after school at home, we only had two short 15 minutes breaks during the day. My sister and I learned the value of being in a new country and learning at our new school. We joined high school clubs and did volunteer work at the hospital on the weekends.

The nuns were very strict and would not let us speak in Indonesian even when we were alone to help us with our assimilation. If we were caught they told us they would hold the mail from our parents for a week. We thought it was very strict, but now I see how we benefited from this approach to being immersed in a new language. Of course, they never held our mail, because we followed the rule, we spoke English everywhere we went. Well, almost everywhere. When we were away from school, like shopping excursions, and it was just the two of us we sometimes spoke Indonesian! My sister and I quickly discovered we had no classes together, this was also so we could learn English faster. The school administration had thought of this, if we had been in the same classes we would have been more likely to do our studies together and not focus on learning English. It was to our benefit. It was important that we were independent enough to rely on our own english skills in our classes. They intentionally wanted us to be separated so we would be forced to try and understand the teacher and everything that went on in the classroom. There was one more reason we were in different classes. Indria focused on math courses which is where her strengths were, while I was more interested in science courses. We grew from this decision now that I reflect back on this time.

We each were assigned a foreign student to aid in our immersion process and Indria and I were not in the same dorm room. Most of the foreign students that were going to our high school were wealthy kids from Mexico. Their purpose in going to Marywood was to become proficient in English, and most had already completed high school. Miranda my roommate, was related to one of the past presidents of Mexico, and her family was very wealthy. She was kind to me and I noticed that she didn't like to study. One day she told me that I was a very good influence on her and I helped her see the value of studying. That was something I remembered and appreciated her telling me.

Everywhere we went we carried a pocket dictionary to help us in communicating. The nuns knew the only way we would learn is to look up the words and then try to say them the best we could. Everyone was very nice and encouraging. Even if they didn't understand us they would simply ask us to repeat what we said so they could help us to pronounce the words correctly. They never put us down or made fun of us and because of their help, we learned very fast. After the first three months, we were communicating much better because of their help. We really appreciated their kindness.

One more thing I liked about my new school and friends, they didn't care if we had a Chinese or Indonesian heritage, they liked us for being us, with no judgment or discrimination. I had no problem explaining my heritage to my friends as I explained how and why my Chinese name was changed. I found most didn't understand why that would have been necessary, and although they were curious, and they respected me for where I came from, it was more important to them to get to know me as their friend. I was well-liked and many of the girls wrote in my yearbook giving me compliments about my study habits, or that I was really nice, and how my sister and I had set a good example for them. The nuns even told us they were proud of us and were appreciative of how we approached our new life. We were just doing what we thought we were there to do, what were accustomed to doing before coming to the US. Work hard, learn as much as possible, and continue to work towards our goals.

In our junior year, I took biology and chemistry, while my sister focused on math courses like calculus. Then in my senior year, I took Advanced Biology. In addition to learning the usual course work, I also had to memorize many English words. In biology class, fortunately, some of the words were in Latin, that was good because I had already studied Latin. I loved the chemistry class and did very well in both classes. It was very evident to everyone that I loved science, especially biology. In fact, my biology teacher, Sister Shirley, nominated me for a science award, and I won it in my senior year.

Both my sister and I did well in algebra, but it was funny because the way we were taught math in Indonesia was different from in the US. The nuns were curious about how we got the correct answers. We were solving the problems differently so we taught them how we had learned and for them it was something new.

Since I was in high school in Indonesia, I have always been determined. Even then, I wrote my goals on a piece of paper and I put it in a drawer and looked at it every day. So when my sister and I came to the US, we made new goals for ourselves. We discussed three main goals. The first was to learn English really well so we could go to college. The Second was, to pass the college entrance exams. And the third was to work hard to get at least a 3.0 grade-point-average so we could get a scholarship. For us, when we first started, we received a D+ in some of our classes. This was very humiliating, so we worked hard to learn English so this wouldn't happen again. To achieve these goals learning English was a main component to our success, and we prioritized them in order of importance.

The dormitory had a study hall for extra study time. However, the nuns were very strict and had go to bed by 10 PM each night. Although we weren't finished studying we had to go to bed anyway. It was sometimes frustrating because I still needed to study after the study hall closed. It was a good thing that I had an understanding roommate. I would study in our room after "lights out' by using a flashlight to read. My roommate was very nice about it and promised not to tell the nuns. I was so determined I needed to study long hours to accomplish the goals I set for myself. Some might have wanted to give up, but I never considered that, because we knew having an education in the United States was the golden opportunity of a lifetime. I have heard people say they need a "why' to reach their goals, ours was knowing our parents, and our siblings who were still in Indonesia were counting on us to start the process and be successful so they could come join us later in the States when it was their turn.

My sister and I were very disciplined and determined and studied very hard to get good grades. When we were in the early part of our senior year, we found out we were qualified to apply for scholarships. I thanked Sister Donna and Sister Shirley for their guidance, which paid off. They helped us identify all of the things we needed to achieve to reach this goal and without them, we wouldn't have known where to concentrate our efforts.

We were enthusiastic students, although it wasn't hard for us because we were always interested in learning more. The teachers loved our enthusiasm for learning! It was a high priority that we showed up early for all of our classes to be able to achieve the success we needed to further our education. We used every opportunity to ask the teachers, the nuns, and our friends' questions, we had so many! We found the girls were very helpful and didn't mind that we asked a lot of questions. We learned to say, "Excuse me, I have to check the meaning of the word in the dictionary." During the lunch break, in the dormitory, between classes, we could be found someplace asking someone a question! They were so helpful and understanding and we were grateful to have them there to help us.

My sister and I started making friends in our new school. We met many more friends in the school clubs that shared our same interests. My sister was in the Math Club and I joined the Science Club in my senior year. I ran and became the Treasurer of the Science Club because I wanted to be in a leadership role. We also joined the Library Club. We later found out that being in extracurricular activities was important to getting scholarships. The girls who became our friends were very nice to us, some of them invited us to visit and stay with them for a weekend. Living in the United States was much better than we anticipated, but we missed our home, our parents, and our siblings. We were very homesick. We learned because we assimilated and respected the American people and culture, and they in turn were very respectful of us and loved our curiosity.

Because we had less than a year to prove ourselves and to apply for scholarships we often politely declined many social invitations in favor of studying. But when Karen Larnard invited us to stay at her home over Easter vacation, it was so nice to go to someone's home and not be left in the dorms. We had a great time meeting her parents and brothers. They asked us several more times to come and visit, but we didn't want to wear out our welcome.

Coming to America had many challenges, one of them was the food. It was very different from the food in Indonesia. It was difficult for us, there were two things we liked in our new country and they were served at the dormitory cafeteria; fried chicken, and pizza. Pizza was already familiar as our American friends in Indonesia would make it for us.

Mrs. B, the cafeteria cook, didn't usually serve rice at our meals. She liked my sister and me and got to know us. She also knew we struggled with the food at times. One day Mrs. B told us, "I have a surprise for you two." We were so excited to find out what it was. She mentioned that she knew we liked rice, so she made us a special breakfast. It was very different from anything we had ever had. There were no rice cookers at that time, and Mrs. B didn't know the traditional way to cook rice with water, so she made it with milk and butter. Similar to the way oatmeal might have been served. We really thought it was awful, but we were also touched that she would go out of her way to make something for us hoping to help us feel at home. She hadn't realized that was not the way we eat rice in our home country. One problem I have, I can't eat too much food that was made with milk. I would have a stomach ache as later on, I found out I was lactose intolerant. My parents had known since I was a child that I couldn't drink fresh milk.

Our friend, Karen let us know if we were missing food from home we could use her kitchen to cook Indonesian foods. So we asked our mom to send us recipes for egg rolls, fried rice, fried noodles, and other things that were simple to make. Karen's parents and her brothers loved the food we made for them while using their kitchen.

We never felt like we were being discriminated against, we believed we felt this way because we made the effort and adopted the culture, and didn't expect to be treated differently.

We were also taught not to swear, and we notice that some of the people we met use swear words often. We didn't know much about the words, as they were foreign to us so we needed to ask what they meant, and when they explained it to us it was very funny, we would get a good laugh!

On the weekends we volunteered at St. Joseph's Hospital as Candy Stripers. We brought lunch to the patients' rooms and this gave us another opportunity to practice our English.

We learned from our parents to be gracious when we ate meals that were prepared for us. We were invited to have dinner with one of my father's business associates who were Americans living in Indonesia when I was a child. The dinner was a roast beef meal, and I really didn't like it. I was asked why I wasn't eating much of the food, and I said I didn't like it. My parent's apologized for my statement. When we got home Dad told me what I said was not the right response in that situation. Dad explained, "Although it may have been the truth, and you might not have liked the food, it is important to appreciate the work that goes into the meal preparation when serving guests". He explained further, "We could tell the host, it's interesting, or I have not had this before. It was always important not to hurt the host's feelings when you are invited to their homes for meals." From that experience, I remembered never to offend the cook!

Our life was full of studying memorization. Because we did not have a great command of the English language it was even harder. Studying American History and literature were difficult. Some of the literature lessons were right after lunch, so it was hard to stay awake and pay attention. When the class was boring and we did not understand "old" English, it was even harder to pay attention. I asked the nun about the words from Shakespeare, the teacher smiled and let me know they were, "Old English" because it is not the same as what was spoken in America. I needed to memorize even more words to understand. I did not comprehend much of what was being said, so it was difficult to stay engaged. We had to study hard, and it took a lot of extra time to learn all that we needed to learn. In spite of the difficulty with school, what made it worth it was the people who treated us with kindness.

When we received notice that we had gotten scholarships for college, my sister and I cried because that meant we accomplished all of the goals we had set for ourselves going into high school. Our hard work had paid off. We called our parents' to share the news, they cried with excitement with us. Back then it was expensive to call long-distance, cell phones had not been invented. We made the call to them because it was important news, not only for us, but it meant my next younger sister could come to the US for her education.

Our graduation from Marywood High School was an awesome and memorable occasion. Both my sister and I graduated in 1971 and we had never had a graduation ceremony before. We wore a cap with a tassel and a gown. Some teachers gave an inspirational speech and then they announced our names and we went to the podium to receive our diploma. I felt very proud of my accomplishment as a high school graduate! Reflecting back and looking at my high school yearbook, many people wrote notes that were very nice. I recall each time I asked one of my friends to sign my yearbook, they were so happy to write a message to me. I couldn't write much in theirs as I was still learning to write in English, but I did my best to respond to their requests. I couldn't write all that I wanted to say to them even though I had come a long way learning English. I was truly grateful for them helping my sister and I.

After Graduation, Karen, my sister and I were invited by my roommate to go to her home in Mazatlán, Mexico. Her family was very wealthy and wanted to host me for the summer before college. Although my sister and I were excited that she wanted us to come to her home, we needed to take some summer courses to further prepare for college. My friend Karen was very delighted to be able to take advantage of the opportunity to go to Mexico with her. Karen felt like I had given her a gift to have an amazing summer. She loved it. She said she was spoiled by all the great food, and it was served by the kitchen staff. She did not have to do any work. She said it was a memorable vacation. I hadn't accepted the opportunity, it was more important that I save money for college, and I knew going to Mexico would cost money. To us it was important to find a job and earn money rather than spending money on a vacation. I was able to save extra money for the following year which really helped.

During the summer I worked at the junior college in the science lab cleaning up, and taking care of the class hamster, and cleaning its cage. Indria and I needed to learn to drive, so we went to driving school. We bought a blue Dodge which was used. It had an eight-cylinder engine and was very powerful to drive.

My parents couldn't both travel to visit us at the same time because one of them needed to stay back to run the art gallery. So Papi came first, for a whole month. We drove my sister to Olympia, Washington where she had been accepted to college. Although it wasn't a vacation to a resort in Mexico, it was a memorable trip, driving from Southern California to Washington with Papi and visiting beautiful beaches and waterfalls. Papi loved the waterfalls in Oregon, the scenery was beautiful. We loved seeing the Golden Gate Bridge. Papi took a lot of pictures so he could paint those beautiful scenic photos at a later time.

We bought a rice cooker so we could cook rice because Papi felt he was not full if he did not have rice with his dinner. While in Hong Kong on a layover, he bought each of us a good Japanese camera with an autofocus feature that made taking pictures easier. He also purchased a portable stereo for each of us. We liked our gifts but the best present was spending time with him. We were so happy about enjoying our summer vacation with him. During the trip, we drove through three states. I liked driving more than Indria, and she was better at navigating. So we made a good team. Although Papi was a good and experienced driver, he let us drive the whole trip, because he said we are more familiar with the rules of the road. It was also because in Indonesia people drive on the opposite side. When it was time to say good-bye to Papi, we were both sad to see him go. Now we were ready for the next chapter of our lives, starting college.

Life Lessons: your reflection

A thought to inspire You:

"I have learned to always take on things I'd never done before. Growth and comfort do not exist." Virginia Rometty

What does this mean in your life? ....

....

....

....

Questions to empower you:

When you experience people from different cultures, do you enjoy getting to

know and appreciate your differences? ....

....

....

....

Did you have a difficult teacher that as an adult you see how they may have

helped you? ....

....

....

Did you set goals early in your life? How did they shape your

future? ....

....

When was a time in your life when you needed to get comfortable with being uncomfortable? ....

....

....

Reflections: what will you apply in your life? ....

....

....

....

....

....

....

....

....

....

....

....

....

"If you don't seek what you want, you will never find it.
If you don't ask, you will never find the real answer."

Angeline Benjamin

CHAPTER 4

Life as a College Student

"The secret of your success is found in your daily routine"
John Maxwell

In my early senior year of high school, I applied for scholarships. I thought, *What do I have to lose?* I found that I was eligible merely because I was a foreign student. I was surprised and excited when I received a full academic scholarship for four years at the College of Notre Dame de Namur in Belmont, California!

The scholarship requirements were they would pay for my education expenses as long as my grade point average was 3.0 and above. This was an excellent help for my parents financially. The scholarship didn't pay for living expenses, so my parents paid for my dormitory. We were all surprised that I received the scholarship, even the nuns.

We later discovered the scholarship I received was not based on financial need, but for academic excellence. My sponsor was Dr. Norman Cousin, who was the editor of The Saturday Review Magazine. Later I was told by Dr. Cousin's representative that I was chosen because of my academic improvement in such a short time. Although my grades suffered when I first came to the United States, I received the scholarship because of the improvement I made and being able to maintain good grades. They also liked that I was active in school activities, and I had worked hard to assimilate to the American culture.

I also received a work grant. My assignment was at the Notre Dame Elementary School, which was located next to the college. My job was to tutor the kids. The teacher I assisted asked me to work with selected students to help them with their English. This was a surprise to me because it was my worst subject at the time. The teacher explained to me that she knew I would work well with the kids because I was very studious, and when she described the job, it was to help the students with spelling. I could do that! I had gotten really good using my dictionary.

During that time, I carried my dictionary with me everywhere. This helped me with the kids because my job was to help them find their spelling words in the dictionary and show them the proper spelling. Even though I was limited in knowing a word's meaning and pronunciation, I was good at spelling and could find words in the dictionary. Occasionally, I was able to help in the science classes also. The school was an all girl's school, and the girls came from families that could afford a private school education. They were polite and referred to me as Miss Benjamin.

The work grant didn't pay me in cash. However, it did pay for the expenses at the dormitory, reducing the costs. This was a big help to my parents! I also worked in the dormitory cafeteria. At that time, it was the best job for me. I chose what foods I got to eat, and I knew what was on the menu every day. The chefs gave me a priority, so I ate before serving the other students. I usually worked during the dinner meal because I didn't have night classes. This job paid money for my personal expenses, like seeing a movie with my friends, going dancing, or other school activities. Sometimes we would go out to dinner. Once, I went to a Karen Carpenter concert. I loved her songs! I could do all these things with the money I earned through my hard work, and not place the financial burden on my parents.

Another job I had was the campus operator during the summer and winter breaks. In those days, the campus operator used a manual switchboard. The switchboard had cords that connected a call between two people. When a call would come in, I would put the phone plugs into the appropriate phone jacks. There was a learning curve, and I disconnected people by accident a few times. It wasn't as easy as it first looked. I learned how to properly greet people and that your first impression was very important.

Sometimes in the evening, I watched the children of a wealthy family. They were very nice to me, and it was one of the easiest jobs I ever had. I got paid mostly just to stay in the house, and I could study, what could be better than that? I would feed the kids dinner and tell them a story, then put them to bed. Then I had the whole night to study! The kids liked me because I sometimes told them stories about my childhood in Indonesia and how I came to the United States. They were very fascinated and wanted me to tell them more. One of the funny experiences I had with them was singing children's songs with them. I didn't know the songs, and they didn't understand why I couldn't sing along. So I told them I didn't sing the same songs as a child in Indonesia, or grow up singing in English. They thought it was funny.

Part of my college success was because I made an excellent first impression with my instructors. I had learned it was important to get to know them, so I would ask them questions about their interests. I found that when I was interested in them, they were more interested in me. When you are excited demonstrate a desire to learn from them the instructors take more interest in helping you all they can. If you don't ask for help and don't make an effort to learn, the professor won't go out of their way to give you extra support.

When I started at the college in my freshman year, I was in the girls' dormitory. The college was a co-ed college. However, it was mostly girls. My first roommate was nice. We didn't socialize because we didn't share the same friends, interests, or classes. We got along great, and we respected each other's privacy. I did not date any men, especially in my Freshman year. My roommate liked to go to parties, movies, and concerts. I could not afford to go, because I didn't have the extra money to spend. I hadn't gotten any jobs yet. She liked history, poetry, and other social activities I had no interest in. I liked science, and she was not interested in it at all. We did not like the same music either. Her taste in men was very different from mine. I looked for clean-cut, intelligent men. She was more into their looks and how popular they were.

My official major was biology, with a focus on microbiology. The school didn't offer a microbiology major, or I would have chosen it. The college, at that time, was known for a teaching credential focus. It was a small college, and I learned a lot. The classes were small, the instructors were attentive, and they spent a lot of time helping them. I wanted to make sure my GPA was maintained to keep the scholarship and graduate within four years. My personal goal was to maintain a 3.3 GPA, that way, I could be on the Dean's List. During my freshman year, I took required classes like Algebra, English, Logic, English Literature, and History.

In my sophomore year, I was able to take more electives. I was in the same dormitory room, but I didn't have the same roommate. My first roommate had moved to the co-ed dormitory with her friends, and Lisa, a Chinese foreign student from Hong Kong, moved in. She spoke English very well. Her goal was to become a dietician, so her courses were in sciences like mine.

She was very outgoing and friendly. We shared many of the same friends. We had mutual respect for one another. She understood why I couldn't speak Chinese because she knew people who had moved to Hong Kong from Indonesia due to the discrimination they faced."

My goal was to become a doctor, so I had to be very dedicated to my studies. My advisor made sure I took a lot of science classes. The only classes I took that were not science classes were required classes, which I needed to graduate.

In my third year of college, Lisa moved into an apartment with another girl because she no longer wanted to live in the dormitory. The main reason was the food. She liked to cook Chinese food, so living in an apartment made sense for her. So I had another roommate for my junior year, and I stayed in the college's apartment, mostly for financial reasons. Living on campus helped me continue to keep the grant.

In my third and fourth year of college, I found a new mentor, Dr. B. as we called him. He was influential in my appreciation and love for microbiology. As a part of my work grant, I was assigned as his assistant, which continued to help with my dormitory expenses. I prepared the materials for the lab and sometimes graded the exams. He told me he once thought he wanted to become a doctor like me and was a medical school student. But then, he found his passion was to teach. He switched from a medical school focus to a microbiology doctoral program, eventually becoming a college professor.

It was through my experiences with Dr. B. that I found my love for microbiology. It wasn't only the way he taught, which was inspiring, but how he made it so interesting. I believe he was responsible for many students falling in love with microbiology because he enjoyed teaching the subjects and had a passion for helping students. I took all of the classes he taught. He was a great mentor and influenced me to follow my passion.

Another college professor Dr. G I really liked her too, and her class was one of my favorites. She was young, very energetic, and well respected. She taught advanced biology and endocrinology. I took both of her courses. One advantage for me, she gave her student oral exams, in addition to a written exam. For me, I thought she was an outstanding professor. She loved to scuba dive. She said I should try it because I was comfortable being in the water. I decided then it was not a good time for me to learn scuba diving.

Although it sounded interesting and I liked water, it was an expensive sport, and also I knew I could not dive deep in the water because it hurt my ears.

One day in the endocrinology class, she told the whole class she was impressed with one student, but she didn't give a name. She explained how disappointed she was with the rest of the class. Because she used the bell curve to determine grades, their performance was compared to one high score. When she gave me my results, I discovered that I was the student that did very well. I was grateful she didn't mention my name to the other students. For me, having the ability to have an oral exam made a big difference. I explained what I knew and had learned when she asked me the questions, rather than memorizing what I learned for a test.

Having time in the science lab was always interesting. My partner was afraid of the rats that we used for our experiments and observations. So I did what I needed to do to complete the assignment, I was almost bitten once, but I loved doing the assignments.

I continued as a pre-med student and loved all of the science classes. I applied for medical school and took biology, chemistry, microbiology, genetics, and anatomy. I took physics, and I liked the theory but not the lab work. Botany was an elective class I took, but I did not care that much for learning about plants. I enjoyed humans and animals more.

The chemistry instructor was an elderly man. He was hard to understand because he didn't enunciate his words. He also had a soft-spoken nature. He made sure he spent time helping us, even after class. At the end of the semester, he invited some of his favorite students to his house for dinner. His wife cooked for us. They did not have children, so I think his students filled a place for both of them. We had fun at his party; we sang and learned new American jokes. We all really enjoyed the evening with them.

During my college years, I did not have any serious relationships. One of my favorite things was to go to dances when they had them. I was not shy and would ask the guys to dance with me because I didn't want to wait to be asked. Because there were more girls than boys at the school when they had dances, boys who weren't students were allowed to attend the dance party. This seemed to make me attractive to some of the men. I think this is why I was never at a loss for dates. I was proposed to twice by two different men. Unfortunately, I just wanted to have a good time, and they seemed to be looking for more than I was willing to give at that time. I knew it would take my full attention to become a doctor. Serious dating and marriage would only be a distraction to my goal.

Occasionally, on the weekends, we would go out to have some fun. I did go to an occasional party, only if I felt good about my school work. I might go on a rare date, or party, sometimes a movie with friends. I also followed the basketball and soccer teams to support the college team, so sometimes I would go to a game. I really enjoyed my college years. Like in high school, I was active in extra-circulator activities. I was a yearbook photographer, an officer in the foreign student club, and later the vice president. I played powder-puff football; everyone was surprised at how strong I was for my height. I also played volleyball. BUT my studies always came first! And it paid off!

I met some interesting men! One was a football player from Stanford. I got to attend all of the home games and met his other friends at the team. He was a nice guy, but it lasted only one semester. He loved football too much and was not serious about studying. He liked to party a lot. The bottom line was he was not my kind of guy.

I met a man at a dance party during my senior year, and I asked him to dance. He was very handsome, polite, courteous, a perfect gentleman, and very intelligent. He was a junior at Stanford and also a pre-med student. We cared for each other and had many shared interests and things in common. We went to many cultural places, concerts, and he took me to try many different kinds of foods. I later found out he came from a very wealthy family. Things were going really well until one day, he told me that he was gay. He was in tears, as he said I was the first person he had ever told. His parents did not even know. He told me he loves me as a friend. He did not want other people to know. That is why he decided to date women, so others will not know. But he told me he could not live a lie dating me. I was touched by his honesty. I told him to follow his true feelings and be proud of who he is. Most of all, I told him he should be honest with his parents and his sister. I told him if his parents love him, they will accept him for who he is. Guess what! He followed my advice and told his family. They were shocked at first but accepted him for who he was. He thanked me and told me I was a true friend. We went separate ways because I graduated but I learned a lot from him!

My philosophy was, put your goals as a number one priority. Most students convince themselves that they need a life outside of their studies. Some got into going to parties, dating, and other things rather than studying. I remember noticing this, especially in my junior and senior years. But that was not for me. I was focused on my studies, not just for my scholarship but also for being accepted into medical school.

Plan B was to go to graduate school if I couldn't get into medical school. I believe you always need a backup plan if your Plan A doesn't work out. Then you know what you will do next, and you won't be disappointed. Although I had a secondary plan, I never thought I would need it.

I applied to five schools with the faith and confidence that at least one of the schools would accept me. I did not apply to state medical schools because I knew the chance of being accepted was very slim to none. Why waste my money! Most students apply for many more, even twenty applications, but the process is expensive, so I sent out fewer applications hoping to get accepted. I applied to Creighton University in Omaha, Nebraska, and Northwestern Medical School in Chicago, Illinois. Taking the MCAT is also expensive, and I didn't want to waste my parent's money.

It was almost impossible to get a medical school scholarship as a foreign student unless you were sponsored or sent by your country's government. Medical school is costly to pay for your education on your own. At that time, being a foreign student, I was not eligible to get a student loan.

They didn't only look at the grade point average, but your study habits. In the interview process, they evaluate you based on many factors. One thing I hadn't realized at the time as they take the students on the standby list and offer them an interview. In this case, there are travel expenses and the possibility of not being accepted.

I applied to graduate school just in case I wasn't accepted into medical school. I applied in the field that I was most passionate about, microbiology. I didn't apply for any state universities, I found it was difficult to get accepted as a foreign student. I would have a better chance to be accepted at a private university. I was not considered a resident in California even though I had lived there. So because I wasn't a resident, they would consider me a foreign student, and it would be difficult to be accepted. My advisor helped me navigate the whole system.

I was accepted to graduate school at the University of Alberta in Edmonton, Alberta, Canada. They even offered a fellowship, for medical microbiology. It seemed like a no-brainer because it would help financially have a fellowship, and I could also apply for a work grant.

By the middle of my senior year, I had all the credits to graduate, so I graduated in December of 1974. By doing this, I also completed my scholarship. I could have continued on for another semester taking classes. However, my concern was my living expenses because the work grant also stopped.

Before I left Notre Dame, I asked three of my professors for a letter of reference. As part of the medical school screening process, I knew these letters would help the colleges learn more about me and the type of student I was. This was one of my strategies to get into a good and respected college. My parents were so proud of my sister and me completing college. Although I graduated early, I still went to the graduation ceremony in June 1975.

My sister Indria met Steve at the University of Washington. He was in the ROTC program and became an officer in the Army. They were making plans to be married and were going to be moving to Huntsville, Alabama.

My sister and I had been sharing the old blue car. When she transferred to the University of Washington, it was expensive for her to keep the car. The parking permit was costly, and also she hardly drove the car because it was easier to take a bus everywhere. So her trusted friend drove the car to California, and I kept the car until I graduated from college. The parking permit at my college was very inexpensive.

My dad made a substantial down payment on a new Ford Mustang for me when I graduated from college as a graduation present. My car was new, and the small monthly payments that I made from working covered the balance. One of my good friends vouched for me so I could get the loan to buy the car. I chose the Mustang because it was affordable, easy to drive, and I liked how it looked like a sports car. I was analyzing each aspect of the purchase because that is how I operate. Then I needed to decide if I wanted an automatic or standard transmission. My friend's husband helped me with the decision. The standard transmission was less money. There was one challenge, I didn't know how to drive a stick shift, but my friend's husband did, so I asked him if he would teach me. It took about a week of his driving lessons in the parking lot for me to feel comfortable driving. So, no problem! I was off and driving the car on my own!

Life Lessons: your reflection

A thought to inspire you:

"The secret of change is to focus all of your energy not on fighting the old, but on building the new." Socrates

What does this quote mean in your life? ....

....

....

....

Questions to Empower you:

What wisdom did your early mentors help you discover? ....

....

....

....

If this was the last day of my life, what would I have regretted? Why? Can

you change? ....

....

....

Am I holding on to anything I need to let go of? ....

....

....

....

Reflections: what will you apply in your life? ....

"Surround yourself with those who see greatness within you,
even when you don't see it yourself."

Angeline Benjamin

CHAPTER 5

Adventures at Graduate School

"If you don't design your own life plan,
chances are you'll fall into someone else's plan.
And guess what they may have planned for you? Not much."
Jim Rohn

After I graduated, while waiting for the June graduation, I decided to do a project that was in line with my desire to be a physician. My mentor, advisor, and favorite professor Dr. B. sponsored my project in a nursing home near the college. Due to a similar college and career path, Dr. B gave me advice that helped me to decide what was right for me. It had been evident to me why he had chosen not to pursue becoming a medical doctor. He was so passionate about microbiology and teaching. His mentoring and guidance helped me decide what right for me. He knew my experience in the skilled nursing facility would help me determine if I had a passion for becoming a doctor. Being in a doctoral program for microbiology would be advantageous for either path I chose.

My experience taking care of the patients, solving their health care needs, and directing their treatment was an opportunity to discover my passion. He suggested for me to try this and then see what I should pursue as a career. I really didn't know what I was going to do at that point.

Because I had graduated, I moved out of the campus apartment and moved into an apartment in Redwood City. Working in a nursing home, I received pay that helped with my expenses. Dr. B. knew this would help me with my decision to become a doctor. The experience was challenging and sad for me, and because of it, I told my parents that I would never put them in a nursing home. It was also in other ways, it was a good thing I worked there for six months.

In the spring, while working at the nursing home, I was accepted into a Fellowship at the University of Alberta in Canada for graduate school. The fellowship was for medical microbiology. I was so grateful.

One of the medical schools I applied for notified me I was on their standby list. Each school only took a set number of pre-med students. Most students send multiple applications and some may receive multiple acceptance letters. They may decide to go to another school. In that case, the students on the standby list are given the opportunity. I was fortunate to be accepted as a standby for Creighton University in Omaha, Nebraska. As a Catholic college, my thought was that I graduated from a Catholic college undergraduate program and would have a better chance of being accepted.

I sometimes wonder if that was meant to be, I likely would have gone and not found what I was genuinely passionate about had I been accepted.

My college years were, without a doubt, some of my favorite years. College was a great experience, one that I am grateful for and that I treasure even today. I wonder about people who couldn't wait to graduate from college because I was sad when I needed to go on to the next chapter of my life.

I really missed my college friends, especially at first. One of my roommates and friends was Maria. I was one of her bridesmaids when she got married. We corresponded for many years. Always talking about getting together for a visit. She worked part-time after retirement and never gave me a time that worked for a visit. Then she found out she had colon cancer, and it spread fast in her body, and she wasn't able to fight back. What Maria's passing taught me was if you want to do something, do it now. There may not be a tomorrow. We always had talked about getting together, and how we would love to take a trip somewhere to catch up, but we never did. My regret is that I never pressed her to tell me when to come. She only lived a few hours away near Sacramento, California. Because I relied on her, I missed getting together with her before she passed away.

One of the highlights of the summer after college was my mom's visit. She came to my college graduation as Papi came when we graduated from high school. So now it was Mom's turn while Papi stayed in Indonesia working in the art gallery. The graduation was very awesome. It was at the cathedral in San Francisco, where the school could accommodate the ceremony with many people in attendance. Our campus was too small. After graduation, we traveled to Seattle, Washington, for my sister's wedding. I was the maid of honor in their wedding. When Mami visited me, I drove the Mustang, for our trip to Seattle. I had wanted to take Mami on a trip like we had done with Papi when we graduated from high school. It was fun, we all enjoyed the trip, and I drove the whole way. My mom didn't drive in Indonesia. Then we drove back to California, and my mom went back to Indonesia.

In early August, I finished my nursing home project and I packed my things. I drove to Alberta, Canada through British Columbia and onto where my new graduate school was in Edmonton. I took my time, enjoying the scenery. I only drove during the day to be safe.

Living in Edmonton was a good experience for me. Especially the weather! Unlike California, Alberta has a very cold, dry winter! In as early as November, there can be snowfall. Once it snowed, we didn't see the ground again until the spring. The temperature could fall as low as minus forty degrees Fahrenheit. Therefore having proper clothing to protect yourself is critical. When I arrived in Edmonton, it was in mid-August, the weather was not freezing cold yet, no snow! I did not have a place to live at first.

Unlike undergraduate school, I was on my own to find a place to reside. I was not able to live on campus because everything was already full. The economy was booming because of the oil industry, so there were few apartments available in Edmonton. To rent an apartment by myself was too expensive. My advisor suggested checking the postings on campus for people looking to share housing. This was my first priority! Find a place to live!

I found a house to share located about a 30-minute drive from the campus. Since I had a car, I could drive every day to the university. I met my future roommate. Her name was Kathleen Murray. She was not a college student but was working full-time in downtown Edmonton. After the interview, I started to like her, she was easy to talk to and very accommodating. Also, I was desperate, I needed a place to stay before classes started. I said to myself, take a chance and go for it! What do I have to lose! I never regretted my decision. I used my instincts and she was a great roommate and true friend. She remains my friend to this today, and we we still hold a mutual respect for each other. She even has the same birthdate as my father! Kathleen, later on, told me she really wanted me to be her roommate too because I was a very serious student and we had things in common. I moved in right away! I accomplished my task and found a perfect place to live.

As winter came, since I have never driven in snow before and the car was from California I needed to prepare the car for driving in cold winters. It already had all-season tires, they were good, most of the main roads in Edmonton were cleared when it snowed. I didn't have a garage, so I needed to have a battery heater. Most of the parking lots on campus had electrical outlets to plug the warmers into, keeping the batteries ready to start. Also at the back of the house, I shared with Kathleen, there was an electrical outlet I used for the car. Kathleen and I had our own bedrooms, she is so kind, she gave me a bigger room. We lived on the main floor of the house, which had a kitchen, dining area, and a living room. The house had a full basement with a separate entrance, a kitchen, and a bathroom, which was rented by another female tenant.

It was very challenging to drive in the snow. Before I could leave to go anywhere it took much preparation. I have to start the car at least 15 minutes ahead of time and scrape the snow off the car. It would take me at least ninety minutes to get to the university so I wasn't late. Because of the classes I took and the research I had to get done, I went to the library between classes. Usually, I got home after dark. In the winter it started to get dark around 4 PM, I usually did not get home until close to seven sometimes even eight.

Driving in the snow at night was a challenge for me. I had to drive a slower speed than most of the local people. My California license plates didn't help! Californians had a reputation for not driving very well in the snow! But what made me decided to stop driving at night in the snow was a near-miss accident. My car spun 360 degrees and almost went off the cliff, had it done so I would have died. I was able to stop the car, just a few feet short of going off the cliff! I decided then, God still wants me to live and so I shouldn't drive at night while I was tired and on my own. I did not tell my parents about the incident until years later. After that incident, I decided to take the bus. The bus stop was just two houses down and across the street. It ran every fifteen minutes in the morning.

My roommate Kathleen didn't know how to drive so she took buses everywhere she went. I decided I would do the same. I stayed at the university for my classes, studying in the library, and eating my meals in the cafeteria because it was more productive. I had the same bus driver whom I got to know him well going home during the week. I learned so much about Alberta and places to visit from him. I did not get a chance to socialize with Kathleen except on the weekend. I spent most of my days at the university. I found out they had an indoor swimming pool that was available for students to use, I took advantage of that because I enjoy swimming. It was a good break for me, two to three times a week. Because I spent so much time on campus, I got a chance to make friends with other graduate students who lived on campus. I befriended graduate students from England, Australia, Hong Kong, Singapore, and Malaysia. Sometimes, I had dinner at the apartment occupied by the graduate students from Malaysia. We socialized with a group of foreign students, mostly men, who liked my cooking.

Throughout college, I had not considered serious relationships and settling down. Being in graduate school now, I was now in a position to consider this. I met two men I really liked, one from England and the other from Australia, I considered having a more serious relationship with them, but neither of the relationships worked out. One of the big reasons was, I did not want to move to England or Australia. However later in my life, I remembered how intrigued I was with their culture and visited these countries.

While in graduate school, I met another mentor, Dr. R. He was so inspiring to me. I was curious about him as he was a medical doctor and a professor in the Microbiology Department. He shared with me his decision-making process of becoming a medical doctor. He found out that he loved teaching microbiology and research. He didn't enjoy patient care. So after he received his medical degree he went back to school to get his doctorate in the field of medical microbiology. Then he began his teaching career at the University of Alberta.

Through my mentors, research, and experience working at the nursing home, I was rethinking my decision to become a doctor. I weighed all of the pros and cons. At this point, I was thinking about all of the conversations I had with professors and heart to heart talks with my mentors. I had decided to become a physician years ago, actually knowing it would take a great deal of time, money, and effort. Was I willing to do these things?

It wasn't easy to change. But I had to admit to myself that I really didn't have the passion for being a medical doctor. I thought if I was a doctor, I could make a lot of money, and my parents would be very proud of me. I knew they had made great sacrifices to help me live my dream. I could take care of them with the money I would be making as a doctor. I spoke to my parents, and they told me not to be a doctor just for them. I needed to follow my dreams. They didn't want me to end up like the professor who became a doctor wasting time and money only to find out it wasn't for him. For me, it was more of financial consideration.

At that time, my professor introduced me to another professor in food science. His name was Dr. T and was from South Africa. He was another inspiring professor. He talked to me about taking his classes. He explained I wouldn't be wasting any time, and it might be something I would like. He was the head of the department, and I could have my fellowship transferred. Knowing I loved microbiology, I decided to explore this area.

I knew I wanted to pursue the opportunity in food science. I loved the subject because it was fascinating, and all people eat, right? I love solving problems with food-borne illnesses, and I thought this would be a valuable career. I really didn't want to take care of patients. It was hard for me to admit this after following this path for such a long time. If you don't make a decision, you could waste time and money. There should be no shame in admitting at some point that you need to change your course.

I was finally able to admit to myself that going to medical school wasn't for me. Sometimes you need to reevaluate. You must dig deep and be honest. Even though you could be embarrassed, it is important to be passionate about what you are doing. In return, your passion and your life are something you will share with others. You will be more fulfilled when you have a career because you want to and not because it is based on your parents' expectations. So I switched my major in the second semester of 1976 and went for a master's degree in food microbiology. Dr. T was able to transfer the fellowship that semester.

Because I was not driving my car that much, I decided to let my sister Indria and her husband use the car while I was in Canada. My Canadian friend and I drove the car to Seattle visiting my two sisters and brother-in-law for Christmas and flew back.

By the spring of 1977, I had completed the courses and was nearly finished with my master's degree program. All that was left was to write my thesis. This is when I found out I had lost my fellowship, due to budget cuts. That and I was not a Canadian citizen. The fellowships were only given to Canadian citizens. At the same time, I talked to my parents, and they had concerns about my brothers' education. They were still in Indonesia, and the political situation had continued to decline.

My plan had been to return to the US after completing my master's program and help my brothers come to the US as my sisters and I had done. My parents were still supporting two of my sisters studying in the US and some of my expenses. It was time to start making decisions about my brothers' future.

My advisor, Dr. T, and I had a long talk. He had left his home in South Africa due to the political unrest, so he understood my families' situation, both in urgency for my brothers and financially. His opinion was that I had all of the knowledge I needed to be a food microbiologist in the field. The only thing that was missing was the title of having my master's degree. I would have benefitted from having a master's or doctorate if I had wanted to teach at the college. But that was not my goal. Working as a food scientist or food microbiologist in the field was not as critical. After taking the time to consider everything, I felt it was a "no brainer."

I spoke to my parents and had a heart to heart talk with them. They knew my family was my first priority. My brothers' safety was an important consideration, and they needed to be in the right environment. My parents trusted me to be their guardian, and it was time for them to come to the US. I was in the best position to help out, and I was the oldest. As part of my Chinese tradition, I felt it was my responsibility to help. My two sisters were in college, and they needed to finish their education. My married sister was moving because her husband was in the military. My goal had always been to return to the US after receiving my master's degree.

There was one more consideration, I was dating a Canadian man that I really cared about who seemed to match my ideals and values, I considered him a long term relationship. He was an electrical engineer and a few years older than me. I had met him at a party hosted by one of my graduate school friends. We were dating when this decision was presented to me. I talked to him about my family and the situation. Although he was not happy with my decision, he understood. He made it clear to me that he had no plans to move to the United States, and I had no intention to stay in Canada.

Carefully considering all of my options, I made a decision and returned to California. I started my career and helped my brothers. My family was more important than the title. I knew I could always go back and finish my graduate program if I wanted. With my brothers, it was a timing issue, and my family was most important. My two brothers needed to learn English and finish high school. I left Canada and returned to California.

Life Lessons:

Reflections to Inspire You:

"In any moment of decision, the best thing you can do is the right thing, the next best thing is the wrong thing, and the worst thing you can do is nothing." Theodore Roosevelt.

What does this mean in your life? ....

....

....

Reflections to Empower you:

What matters most to you in your life? ....

....

....

Do you make decisions based on your values? ....

....

....

....

Have you made sacrifices based on knowing it was the right thing to do and

how did it impact you? ....

....

....

....

....

Reflections to apply in your life: ....

....

....

....

....

....

....

....

....

....

....

....

....

....

*"Make sure you don't start seeing yourself through
the eyes of those who don't value you.
Know your self-worth even if they don't"*

Angeline Benjamin

CHAPTER 6

Goal Accomplished Family Reunited

"Recalling a special moment
allows you to draw on the extraordinary energy
from which you can make your dreams come true.
I call these butterfly moments. "
Lori Raupe

Back in Indonesia, the political issues in the country continued. So I decided to help my parents by bringing the last two of my siblings, my only brothers, to the US. I went back to the United States from Canada in the spring of 1977. I found a condominium in Tustin, near the High School. My brothers would be getting an excellent education there. I became their legal guardian and was responsible for them as far as the school was concerned because they were both underage. All of the documents that needed a parents' signature, I signed. I didn't mind this at all, and they didn't mind me being their guardian. They were happy to be in the US.

At that time, Johan was 14, and Wendel was 17, and in January 1978, they arrived in California with Mom. It had been a long time since I had seen them, and I had missed them all. There had been no school for the holidays in Indonesia, they are off for the whole month of December, and in January, school resumes. So right after Christmas was a good time for them to come. My mother came with them, just in case, there were any problems on the way into the States because they were not adults.

My brother, Wendel, started into the junior year of high school, just as my sister and I had done, repeating a grade in America. This was to give him more time to acclimate, and assimilate into the culture and learn English. Both Johan and Wendel took English in Indonesia, but this gave them more time in high school to prepare for college.

As their guardian, I spoke to the principal about Wendel to make him aware of how important it was for him to get accepted into college. This would give him eighteen months to be ready. The principle and his advisor agreed with the plan, and they were pleased I was advocating for him.

I really enjoyed living with my brothers, I had missed them all so much, and my brothers had grown since the time I had last seen them in 1972 when I returned home for a short vacation and to have dental surgery. Because I did not have dental insurance, so it was less expensive to get it done in Indonesia. At that time, Johan was only 9, and Wendel was 12.

We all had chores to do, clean, cook, and make the beds, dishes, and everything was assigned. I set a schedule for all of us to get everything done. I learned not to expect people to know what they have to do or be accountable for unless you take the time to explain their duties and consequences.

They were happy to be in the US, and the expectation was for them to stay out of trouble because if they caused any problems at school or with the police, they would be sent back to Indonesia. They rode the bus to school, and on some days, I would take them before I went to work. They were never in any trouble. I was pleased with them and grateful they chose good friends. They stayed out of the drug and alcohol culture, and focused on their studies instead.

Wendel graduated from high school as expected and was accepted into a two-year college in Wyoming. One of my father's friends in the art business, sponsored him, and was very helpful. Wendel was very independent and enjoyed a quiet life. Wyoming seemed perfect for him. So both my brothers and I took a road trip. Wendel being an outgoing and independent person made many friends and did well.

Johan was less independent than my brother Wendel. As his guardian, I attended his parent-teacher conferences. They confused me as a high school volunteer because of my young age, which I found amusing. All of his teachers told me he was very smart and enjoyable to have in their classes. I had no doubt he would be able to attend college.

The Art Gallery

Once back in California, I went to our attorney for advice about my citizenship process. The attorney explained I could not work without residency. I needed a green card. Although I had intended to pursue a job in microbiology. I couldn't until I had gone through the residency process. One option was for me to start a business. There were requirements that I could fulfill as a business owner, it made sense to look into opening an art gallery. Because I graduated from a high school in the States, and I could speak English, I could open a business if it was unique to the United States. I personally didn't have my Dad's artistic ability, but I did appreciate fine artwork. I loved having the art around me and knew its history. I could talk to people about art and run the business. It all made sense at the time.

The art gallery was in Tustin and was my full-time business. I had brought some of the fine pieces with me from when I had taken a vacation in Indonesia. Also, my dad and my mom brought some artworks with them when they visited us. I had never disclosed to anyone that the art in my possession was expensive original art from famous artists in Indonesia. Some of the artwork I didn't display but kept in a safe place. I thought once I had a home, I would want to display it then.

In the art gallery, we had pieces from artists that I knew including their history and favorite art mediums. We had a variety of pieces, like oils, acrylic, watercolor, copper, even feathers. We also had woodwork and bone carvings. Even though I'm not an artist, I really enjoy and appreciate art. I learned this from my father. The only difference between my father and me was that he never sold art. He was a storyteller and people wanted to buy the art because of the story. With me, I was an educator and not a storyteller like my Dad.

After I obtained my US residency, I needed to reevaluate the Art Gallery's financial status. I went back to the Larnards' to consult about what to do with the art gallery. I found out our artwork was of good quality, so that wasn't the problem. However, we were in the wrong location for Indonesian art. The art was for a particular clientele and was unique. It was not for everyone's taste. The location in Tustin was not right for our business. I also learned the importance of marketing. I had not been marketing our art gallery, so no one knew we were there. The bottom line was it wasn't profitable and it had served its purpose.

After taking a business course at the junior college, I learned another part of the business that I didn't have in place which was a marketing strategy. Marketing is very important, no matter how good your product is, if no one knows about it, you won't be profitable. Years later, these things came to light as I thought about what I had learned by having the art gallery. I also learned what was successful in Indonesia may not be successful in the US.

About the time we evaluated the business, the landlord increased the rent, and the insurance was also expensive, so we decided to close the gallery. The final thought that helped me decide to close the gallery was I needed financial independence from my parents, as they were still helping me with the business. I wanted to help my parents and help my brothers, which wasn't going to be how I could help them. It was sad to close the gallery, yet this caused me to look at options that were in line with my dreams.

We had a closing sale and sold many of the art pieces, and the rest we saved them. We saved some of the paintings that meant a lot to all of us. I was ready to start my career in microbiology.

Our Family Reunited

My parents came to the United States in 1980. They were sponsored by my sister Indria. It was an emotional experience to have them finally join us. We acknowledged their sacrifices and how they worked so hard to provide for my siblings and me to have an excellent education and a good life in the United States. It was now their turn to live in and acclimate to our new adopted country. They sold everything to move; their home, belongings, and business in Jakarta. I didn't realize at the time how difficult it was for them to move, both emotionally and mentally difficult. They left a lifetime of friends and their families. My mom especially found it challenging. She knew some English but needed to learn how to communicate better, which was difficult.

One of my friends shared her experience moving her parents as we were doing, and just how difficult it had been. Imagine having new foods, a different culture, missing your friends and family. Her parents found it was so complicated they had returned to their country.

My parents assimilated despite challenges. I really admired their fortitude. The most important thing for them was to be with us, their children. Moving to a foreign country is hard no matter your age, but it is more challenging when you are older. They were 55, and they had to learn many things all over.

In Indonesia, my parents had people who helped them with childcare and housekeeping. This was a tradition for people of a certain status, and in exchange, they had their room and board provided for them, besides receiving a salary. My parents provided a great life for their domestic help compared to what they previously had. Often the people that worked for other families did so to give their families a better life and a better education. The household help always cared for us and did the hard work. The homes needed continual cleaning because of the humid weather. Also, there were no modern appliances.

In the United States, my parents didn't have the extra help, which was a big adjustment. So my dad learned to help my mom with the housework and grocery shopping, among other things. Especially with cleaning the house, my mom was asthmatic, we did not want her to do a lot of physical housework, and my dad was very neat and wanted his home to reflect this.

When I came to the States, I didn't know how to do laundry, cook, or do the everyday things one would know if you didn't grow up with household help. My parents' focus was not for their girls to learn to be a wife but to be educated.

Because things were so foreign, they bought a home in Lake Forest, CA, and my brother Johan and I lived with them to help them get to know where things were and make the necessary adjustments. Papi had more time on his hands because he was adjusting to retirement.

Our residency was critical, so my sister and her husband sponsored my parents. I was also getting my residence at the same time. It was wonderful to have my parents in the United States with us. We had finally united once again. It had been a long time since we had lived together. They were very understanding that I was already an adult and independent and knew how to get around. I didn't need to ask permission, but I kept them informed of what I was doing so they didn't worry about me. We needed to care for them until they were comfortable. I was their driver, taking them to the places they needed to go until my dad received his driver's license.

One of my mom's learning experiences was when she went shopping on her own one day. Being a resident, she felt she couldn't buy just anything. I didn't understand her concern, but then it dawned on me in Indonesia, the Chinese didn't have the same rights as the Indonesians. She thought because she was only a resident, she didn't have the same rights. I needed to explain, this is America, you can buy anything you want! Being in the United States, I never felt discriminated against. Many people welcomed me with open hearts and open arms, as they did for my parents.

To my parents, being a resident in America meant they needed to speak in English. They spoke English the best they could whenever they were away from their home. This was an expectation they had taught us many years before, assimilate, learn to speak in the country's language, and not to expect that they should learn our language or culture. Little did we know there was no official language at that time, although it was an assumption.

Life Lessons: your reflection

A thought to inspire you:

"Adaptability is not imitation. It means the power of resistance and assimilation." Mahatma Gandhi

What does this quote mean in your life? ....

....

....

....

Reflections to Empower you:

How have you adapted to new circumstances in your life ....

....

....

....

What are the values you use as a filter for your decisions? ....

....

....

How have you empowered others to help you with the things that needed to

be done? ....

....

....

....

Have you worked for years to accomplish a goal? How did you do it, and what did you learn along the way? ....

....

....

....

Reflections: what will you apply in your life? ....

....

....

....

....

....

....

....

....

....

....

*"Focus on what you want and the rewards you will enjoy
rather than what you don't want
and then be paralyzed by fear."*

Angeline Benjamin

CHAPTER 7

My Professional Career

"Your chances of success in any undertaking can always be measured by your belief in yourself."
Robert Collier

First, let me explain my interpretation of a traditional scientist. Scientists deal with facts and research, and they do not necessarily engage with people. Scientists research, test, review, investigate, and document. They deal with a few people, and they need little or no people skills to do well at their job. The people factor is not an important factor.

Now I can explain the meaning of a non-traditional scientist using science as the basis, and that is where the similarities stop. You also need to factor in the risks and benefits and also use common sense. In this type of science, there are grey areas. As a non-traditional scientist, you also use your common sense to solve problems and other known scientific or problem-solving techniques and emotional intelligence. In this role, there is a necessity to understand people, not just human behavior, but also how to engage and interact effectively. Non-traditional scientists also use facts and research. However, they commonly interact with people to gather information and solve problems.

One other significant differentiation, there is a grey area in non-traditional scientists. Whereas in traditional science, typically, there is no grey area. Decisions are based on risks and benefits, along with other variables. This has been not only my expertise but also my passion. To be effective in this role, I needed to know more than mere microbiology or science facts. I also needed more skills to be effective, especially in the area of risks and benefits. Anytime you have people involved, it has more challenges in my jobs with quality assurance.

My parents and Karen's parents the Larnards, supported my dream. With their support, I prepared for my first professional career, the first thing was a resume. I got advice from Mr. Larnard, who was a business owner. After my resume looked professional, I searched the classified ads in the newspaper. At that time, there were no internet job websites. I found a job listing for a microbiologist laboratory technician at Hunt Wesson Foods. It was a perfect fit for me and my education. The skillset they needed was plating bacteria to isolate, identify, preserve, and destroy it when necessary. I would use the skills I had developed while I was in graduate school, so I felt confident in this area.

This was my first professional interview, so I wanted to make sure that I was there on time and prepared for the interview. I knew it would be crucial for me to ask for what I wanted. This took courage, and I was nervous. Later on, I realized I had used the same philosophy I used previously. What do I have to lose? When I applied for my college and graduate school scholarships.

I wanted to be prepared, I knew that would help me more than anything, confidence mixed with experience, that was a winning combination! I asked Mr. Larnard what type of questions would they likely ask in a job interview. They were helpful and gave me many questions that I used to in preparation. I wrote them out and then decided how I would answer each one. After that, I practiced my responses in front of my mirror.

My dad and Mr. Larnard let me know that my body language needed to show my confidence, and I needed to dress for success. They told me to always dress a level higher than the job you were applying for. Even though the job was a technician, I dressed conservatively as a manager or supervisor might have. I wore a basic suit. My passion for being a microbiologist was now going to be fulfilled. I kept a positive attitude and envisioned them, offering me the job.

I was excited when they called to schedule an interview. The job listing asked for a minimum of two years working in a lab, and I included my experience as a graduate student, which I hoped would apply to the requirements. The interview went very well, I felt good about it, and I was nervous. However, I was confident in my body language, and in my responses to the interview questions, I had dressed for success, I put into motion all that I had been taught.

The following day I received a call for another interview. This time it was with a higher level management team, and again the interview went well. I was a pro by now, or so I thought! With all of this experience in front of the mirror and in-person, I felt like I was experienced.

They offered me the job the following day. When I received the call, I was both surprised and excited. I learned that all of my preparation paid off, and even though my experience wasn't exactly what they wanted when you take action and reach for what you want, you will get it. And if you don't get the job, then so what? You just try again. It is essential to ask questions and show confidence and interest in what you want.

Getting the Job

Once I got the job, I asked my supervisor why he hired me. He said it was because of how I answered his last interview question. I remember his question well, "Why should I hire you?" I had prepared for this question. I remember my response, I said very confidently, "I am a fast learner, I am good at what I do, and I can quickly learn this job. Just give me one month to prove myself, I will prove it to you, without your disappointment. If I am not able to the job, you can fire me and I will leave. You will not need to put me on probation because I did not fulfill my commitment." He added, "I knew you met the criteria, but when you were confident with your responses, you were open and honest with your answers, and confident that you could do the job, I made my decision right then."

When I started the job, my goal was to be promoted within six months. I didn't want to be a lab technologist for long. I didn't mind starting on the bottom. And as a new employee, I wanted to prove myself. Although it was hard for me to get up early, because I am a night person, I showed up at work early every day. I took ownership of my job. I made sure I did everything correctly and any mistakes I corrected as I was able. I didn't blame anyone, because it was my mistake. I worked until the job was finished each day. I didn't leave at five just because the clock said it was time to go home. I made sure the work was completed.

After one month, I fulfilled my promise to prove myself, my supervisor told me that I had exceeded his expectations. During my evaluation, I asked my supervisor what the qualifications were to be a supervisor. I knew this would show my interest in promoting. I already knew the qualifications, and I knew I could do the job. I had previously discovered a supervisory position was open, and I wanted the promotion. I was prepared before I asked the question.

My supervisor told me later that he was pleased that I asked about the promotion. It showed initiative. So I asked for the promotion I had been preparing for by doing the duties even without the title or pay. My supervisor was favorable to the idea of promoting me. He told me he would consider me as a candidate when they are ready to fill the position.

Three months after getting my first job, I was promoted as a lab supervisor. My goal was fulfilled. This was when my career in quality assurance began. I learned from my supervisor, being in charge wasn't the only thing I needed to do. I needed to set an example, and I needed to take care of the people who worked for me. I was happy to work as hard in my new role as a supervisor, as I had to show my commitment when I first began my career with them.

Laid Off

While working at Hunt-Wesson, I had been comfortable. My boss knew me and my capabilities, so this was a bonus. I was aware of my accent throughout my career, this and being a woman could be a hindrance. I knew I would not always be a good fit. It helped to work with people who knew my abilities and supported me.

One way to promote in my field might require me to change companies. I had observed others leave for better opportunities. It helped me understand and was certainly something I would consider.

During the time I worked for Hunt-Wesson, I had a good mentor and manager. After a few years, he moved to Denny's Restaurants Corporate Offices. He asked me if I would go with him. He was setting up the people around him that he knew were capable of supporting him. Taking on a new position in a new company forced me to get out of my comfort zone again. It was a good job, and I knew it. And I had the support of someone I had previously worked with, this made the job more desirable. I was excited and thrilled to be offered a promotion with a new company. So I followed my manager's lead by accepting the promotion in the lab as a Quality Assurance Technology Supervisor.

In my new job, I was required to travel. I got to see the country, and I enjoyed seeing the cultures in different towns, seeing the country and meeting new people.

In my new position, I was learning new things. I audited the product suppliers and also the warehouses. This was new to me. I was also learning new areas in product development, writing product specifications, and learning to develop product identification with a focus on writing policies and procedures. I was required to review a lot of data. I really felt it was a good move for me, and I was making a better income.

At this point in my life, I decided it was time to buy my first home with the income I was receiving, rather than rent. The good thing, the timing was right. I was a first-time homebuyer, and I received financial advantages, so I used my 401K account to make the down payment without penalty. I purchased a new condominium in Mission Viejo. I received better tax breaks and a special interest rate.

My new home was a one-bedroom with an extra room for an office or guest room. I was proud of myself for being able to be a homeowner. My family was happy. Also, they knew they had an extra room when they came to visit. My sister, Indria, had two children by this time, so she was excited that they had a place to stay with me when they visited.

Things were going really well. One day my manager left Denny's and accepted a job at Taco Bell. This was a surprise to me. The next thing that happened, my director was laid off, then my co-workers were laid off. It was all very interesting as I saw it unfold around me. I was told it was due to a buy-out which had happened a few months before.

There were more and more people leaving, especially at higher levels. Eventually, I was the only one left in quality assurance. My thought was to keep doing a good job, so I could keep my job. One day the manager from product development asked me to come to her office. She was in tears as she told me she needed to lay me off. I was really shocked, but she assured me that it had

nothing to do with my performance. An outside consultant had made a recommendation due to the financial condition of the company. I was crushed. I took it as being fired, and I had never been fired in my life! It was difficult to turn over everything I had worked so hard to develop to a person junior to me. No matter what my manager said, it felt like I was a failure. The only thing that made it better was the severance package that I received.

The director, who had also been laid off, spoke to me. She had been a good mentor. She explained it was common in the corporate world. Every time there is a merger, or one company takes over another, the people are at risk. The higher you are in the corporate structure, the more at risk you are. It wasn't a personal thing, it was just business.

The previous director was able to find a good job working in another company. She told me everyone knew what was happening at Denny's, so they would understand that it wasn't me or my performance, just the merger. She told me not to worry. It did make me feel better; however, it still was a time of uncertainty!

My parents were very supportive. They reminded me I was intelligent and not a quitter. They told me I would find a job in no time. At that time, I thought, of course, my parents would always be proud of me and support me. Looking back now, I consider myself blessed to have my parents.

The severance package gave me three months of wages and the ability to use an outside consulting company like human resources personnel to revise my resume and take advantage of interview coaching. I could go to their office every day for help looking for a new job. Another good thing, before I left Denny's, the vice president of my department came to talk to me. He assured me that I had done a good job for them, which he documented in a recommendation letter that I could use when applying for new positions. It was an extraordinary gift. After reading the letter, I was very emotional with all of the things he said about me. He personally signed the letter, and because he was concerned for me, my confidence began to return. Everyone had told me it wasn't me, but this unsolicited act of kindness was important for me to see the truth of the situation.

After that, I thought, *I don't have time to feel sorry for myself!* I better get going and get a new job. I knew the severance pay would run out sooner than later, and with my cost of living expenses, which included my new mortgage payment, I couldn't waste any time.

Mr. Larnard had been looking for someone to help him in his business doing some special projects. He told me that he needed someone like me to help him because I was dedicated to my work. He had been looking but hadn't found anyone. I felt much better. Rather than spending my severance pay, I earned income.

My focus was on practicing my interview skills. Every time a job was posted, I submitted my resume and showed up for interviews. I found that the interview experience helped me improve each time. If something didn't go well, I improved for the next interview.

When I wasn't looking for a job, I was working with Mr. Larnard. He understood about the time I needed off to go for interviews and apply for jobs. He saw my diligence, and he also knew that it wouldn't take me long to find something with my dedication. He did make one request of me. He asked if I could stay with him for at least one month to get his projects completed if I was offered a job. We both knew that when I would be offered a new job, they would typically let you give notice to your current employer before committing to the start date. I thought his request was very reasonable. Of course, I agreed.

Almost one month later, I was called to interview with Carnation. Nestle was the multinational parent corporation, a food and drink processing conglomerate that bought out Carnation as a subsidiary. It was a Swiss-owned corporation and the largest food company in the world. Nestle is most known for chocolate.

The position they were looking to fill was a Plant Quality Assurance Manager. The description included designing a new lab, developing policies and procedures for the operation, and hiring the staff. It had not been built yet. I would also oversee the day to day quality assurance operation and sanitation departments. The only challenge I saw at that point was the location of the plant, which was in Montebello, California. This was not the best area to work in or to live. It was a small plant purchased from Pasta and Cheese, a small company that produced fresh pasta and sauces. I was excited to learn another part of the food services industry. So I interviewed for the job.

I was no longer an inexperienced entry-level employee. I was experienced running a Quality Assurance Lab, being a field Quality Assurance auditor, writing specifications, and product development. One more important skill I had acquired was the art of coffee tasting. While I was at Denny's, I was trained in this skill. They look for a taster that is not a coffee drinker, and you need to have the skills to identify the flavor nodes in the coffee. This bit of information added levity to the interviews.

With a new position at Carnation, I would be adding new areas of expertise and the challenge of new opportunities. I really liked that idea. The day after the interview, I was called for a second interview. They seemed excited about me at that time, they took me for a tour, and I interviewed with another manager. Afterward, they offered me the job.

I talked it over with my parents, Mr. Larnard, and the consultant. Mr. Larnard and the consultant both told me I should have in mind the salary I wanted. I was surprised at what they thought I should ask for. It seemed like a lot more than I was making previously, nearly fifty percent more. They said for my experience, what the job would entail, the knowledge required, and the responsibilities, it should be that amount. It was more than they told me they were going to pay, the consultant said, "Be confident and firm, they are already offering you the job." I thought, What do you have to lose?

After the consultation, I wrote an acceptance letter with a proposal for a greater salary. They needed to take it under advisement. A few days later, I received a call. The Vice President of Operations in the Corporate office wanted to have a talk with me. I dressed as if I already had the position, I wore a suit, and I practiced my interviewing skills once more.

I drove to Los Angeles for the meeting. He was a charming man from Switzerland. He seemed like a firm person, committed, disciplined, focused. I thought we had this in common with a similar personality. We had a conversation for about an hour, he asked many questions, and I also asked many questions. After the meeting he concluded, "Congratulations, Angeline, we are pleased to accept your counter offer. When can you start?" I tried not to show too much excitement, but I was thrilled! I thought to myself, Wow, okay, I didn't expect an answer so quickly.

Later, I figured they must have wanted to see what they were getting for that amount of money. Or maybe they would counter again. I let him know I had been laid off from Denny's, and he remarked that it was Denny's loss. He couldn't wait for me to start working. I also let him know about the commitment to Mr. Larnard, and I needed to complete the projects as promised, and I didn't want to let him down after his kindness. He told me that it was very reasonable, and it was no problem.

With much of the severance pay still in the bank, I was so excited. I called everyone to share the news. My parents were so excited for me, my sisters and brothers were excited, Mr. and Mrs. Larnard, were all excited for me. I was so down just a few weeks before. Now, I was on top of the mountain! I couldn't ask for more than that! The new position was a good career move in a new industry, and a new adventure and all with more money! I moved up after being laid off!   Getting laid off was hard. But I learned that people appreciate confidence and understand someone wanting to get paid for what they are worth. Confidence is very important.

A New Opportunity

At Pasta and Cheese, to be effective in my job, I needed to spend time with the people working for me. I took pride in being diligent in my work. It was very important, not only for myself, but that was the expectation. One thing that was aggravating to me was when I ran into lazy people. My job entailed working with corporate officials and line workers, and everyone in between. I would work a variety of shifts to observe all parts of the operations. Being at the plant for all the shifts was a challenge to me. Although I was told I didn't need to do it because there were supervisors on duty, I still felt that to be an effective manager, I needed to fully understand and meet the people who worked for the company, and specifically for me.

It was vital for me to have everyone know who I was. My typical shift was the day shift, the same as the corporate hours. I did have one unique project. In fact, it was what I was hired to accomplish. I was hired to build a relationship with the United States Department of Agriculture (USDA) inspector. Because we manufactured food for the general public, we received regular visits from the USDA inspectors. This was the law. We needed to be in compliance before production, during production, and after production.

One of my responsibilities was to work with the USDA inspector. Because, The plant produced highly regulated foods, classified by the government agency as "potentially hazardous foods" If the inspector found serious food safety issues, the plant can be shut down by the inspector.

Mr. Adam was my boss and the plant manager. He explained that the USDA inspectors were very unreasonable. He was from New York, very expressive, and used a lot of swear words. After I got to know him, I did have an opportunity to let him know his foul language really bothered me. He was shocked and told me no one had ever said that to him. I asked him to refrain when I am around or when he was talking to me. He apologized and told me he really didn't mean anything by it. He used the excuse that he was brought up with that language, so it seemed familiar to him. I let him know I was not brought up that way. We had an understanding after that, and he did respect my request. We also got along very well, and we honestly had many conversations. We both cared about the company. My number one job was to keep the production going with food safety in mind, and he understood that. I took my previous experience with me to solve the issues at this plant. After working with the USDA inspector assigned to our company, I realized he had a big ego, as described by Mr. Adam. So my best approach was to put my active listening skills to work.

In our first meeting, I approached him so that I was there to resolve the past problems. In general, inspectors don't like to be challenged. If you approach them with an attitude of being sincere and open to learning what they are looking for and intend to correct any infractions right away, they are not as difficult.

The inspector asked me for a few things. He asked for a special parking place near the entrance door. I honestly didn't see any reason to grant his request. However, in the spirit of wanting him to feel we valued his time when he visited the plant, I received special approval to ensure he was given his own parking space. We also made it clear to everyone that no one would have permission to use it, including the corporate managers, when they came for a site visit.

The inspector's second request was that he would not be ignored while at the plant. He wanted the staff to show him courtesy and respect when he came for the inspections. This also was an easy fix for me. I was there now, and I would walk with him whenever he came for inspections.

The third request he made was to have a private locked office at the location. He needed the office to do his work, have privacy to get his job done. It was understood that the office space and also office furniture came at a premium. The plant manager did not feel that a person that might come two or three times a week deserved an office. He thought it was wasted space, and although the inspector was allowed to use an office when he was there, it had not been private, and other corporate officials had also used this, which upset the inspector. So I made sure we gave him the office. I had only two keys made, one for him and one for myself. No one was to use the office except him. This was a goodwill gesture for our company to make for him, and actually an easy fix.

After my first meeting with the inspector, I instructed Mr. Adam to let me deal with him. Stay away from having interactions with him that might inflame the situation, and only when I asked him to answer questions would we need his input. After a few weeks, I was successful at building rapport with him. He was happier, and his whole attitude changed just by giving the three things he requested. Mr. Adam felt that I had used my womanly charms to make the inspector happy. I explained to Mr. Adam that was not the case. I gave him three things. They were an easy fix. I spent time with him to answer his questions. He didn't need to wait for the things he asked for. I did my job, and let him do his. Over a few months, we saw him less and less. Production was not interrupted anymore, and that was good for the bottom line. The Vice President of Operations was pleased with how I was able to keep the inspector happy, even Mr. Adam was happy. We no longer had issues with the inspector.

My next project was new to me, but I could draw from the previous experience I had gained while I was working at Denny's Restaurants. Then, I needed to audit our suppliers. Now I was on the other side, but it wasn't complicated or foreign to me. I was surprised to find out that the company didn't have a product receiving program. The proper protocol was to inspect and test the product before accepting them into the inventory for use. I used my previous experience of auditing to set up a policy for the product receiving department.

For example, eggs are considered a potentially hazardous food. If they are not adequately taken care of, the product could make the end-user sick. They needed to pass inspection. Any delays could hold up production. Because the plant did not have a lab to test the raw material. I set up a procedure, upon delivery, certain foods must be sent immediately to the lab via courier. It was essential to rush the testing, and when done correctly, there was no delay in production.

Another mandatory program that needed to be in place was testing potential hazardous bacteria in the finished vacuum-packed products before being released to the consumer or distribution center. If the product was vacuum packed, it must be tested right away. It couldn't be forgotten about. Otherwise, the products would be placed on hold, which delayed production processing. I needed to get a policy in place and then educate the production managers to make sure they understood.

Many things were not in place because the company had been a small mom and pop establishment before Carnation Corporation taking it over. The quality assurance processes were not in place, so the workers needed to be educated. Then I wouldn't get any push back from anyone. The plant manager and I worked very well because he understood my role in the food's safety. The production manager and the receiving manager hadn't understood why I was involved in their areas. Their initial impression was that this small Asian woman could be easily manipulated, and they thought they could take advantage of me. When I didn't let them push me around, they didn't like me much, and they started to rebel.

Again I needed to use the skills I had developed to build rapport. After all, we were all on the same side. Another challenge I had to face was working with older male line employees. The management had no problem with me, but the older men who had seniority were more difficult to persuade and weren't cooperative. They thought they should be first in line for promotions, but I refused to use that policy. Sure all things being equal, seniority would prevail, but there was also merit. This caused problems. I thought they were male chauvinists. My nickname became "dragon lady." The women workers really respected me and thanked me many times because I brought a refreshing and welcome change to the workplace. They thought it was good that if they worked harder, they would have a chance at the promotions because many were better at their performance and compliance than the "Good Ol' Boys Club."

One of my duties was to educate. The plant had several union workers, and one misunderstood perception was that union workers were protected and couldn't be fired. I refused to accept this belief. My job was to make sure everyone was educated in food safety, and no shortcuts were allowed. If you came to work under the influence or stole things from the company, these offenses were automatic terminations. I also added that if someone willingly took shortcuts in food safety, they too would be terminated. I allowed one verbal warning. The issue must be corrected right away. However, if the same problem occurred, a written violation would be issued for the infraction, but that was all. I explained to them that one shortcut could cost the company millions of dollars in lawsuits and cause deaths from food-borne illnesses. This was an important issue, but foreign to them as they had not previously worked under the strict guidelines. It was a continual message that I needed to ensure everyone understood. Some never got the point and so faced repercussions.

Dealing with the union stewards and representatives was another group that seemed to be a constant battle. They defended the members that neglected their duties. I needed to educate them also. I explained why the USDA inspector was there so often, even two or three times a week doing inspections. Shortcuts could lead to deaths. Most of the workers eventually got it. If the staff didn't follow food safety policies after the first verbal warning and a written violation, I terminated them. I needed to terminate two people because they hadn't learned after the warnings I gave them. Both were senior employees, and the union was involved. The employees felt that it was forgivable because it had never happened to them, and no one had held them accountable in the past. In their eyes, it was okay to do things the same way as before. They also believed that because they were in the union, they couldn't get fired. I prevailed. They learned the hard way and had to find another job. It was something I knew the company couldn't play around with because it only takes one shortcut for a disaster to happen. This is where I always needed to evaluate the risks and benefits. If an employee was too great a threat, they had to go. It was that serious.

After the first year I was there, a consultant came to evaluate the cost of adding a quality assurance lab. They decided it would be too costly to do so. Rather than expand in Montebello, they decided to expand the plant in South Carolina and close the Montebello plant. They offered me a position in the new location and to move me there. I said I would consider it, but I wanted to visit the town to see if it was a place where I would consider living.

It was a nice newer plant with all of the quality assurance programs in place. But there were some insurmountable issues. I was a single woman, so I needed to evaluate the entertainment, the nightlife, and the restaurants. I needed to know what my social life would be like. The town was small, only one movie theater. Not only that, but only a few restaurants, and no Chinese or Asian options for eating out. And I love Asian Food. I would have made more money there due to the cost of living. It was not a promotion or a raise. California is an expensive place to live, and Orange County has an even higher cost of living than in most California cities. One even more important factor in the decision was my parents. I wanted to spend more time with them as they were getting older, not less time. I had lost so much time being with them earlier in my life when we were in separate countries. I couldn't overcome that. I turned the job down and explained why to the Vice President of Operations. He was an understanding man but didn't know how he would replace the "Dragon Lady."

With my work experience, I knew I would have no trouble finding a new job. My parents were happy. I was not going to move. Mr. Larnard had a project for me again, and it would only take me about a month to complete. I told him, no problem, I could commit to a month. Carnation laid me off and gave me severance package and a generous bonus that I had earned.

I wanted to take a well-deserved vacation before looking for a new job. It was nice to know that I could work for Mr. Larnard after my short vacation. Also, Mr. Larnard told me, after I completed my one month project, if I hadn't found a job, I could stay longer until I found a job. So I went on a vacation, this time I was traveling alone to Club Med Caribbean for a much needed break.

Another Opportunity

Once I returned, I discovered both Taco Bell and Burger King were looking for a Field Quality Assurance Manager. Taco Bell called first, and then Burger King called the next day. The headquarters for Taco Bell was right near my home, so that was very convenient. I got the feeling after the first interview they really wanted to hire me. The job at Burger King might have required me to move to Florida. I interviewed with the Director of Quality Assurance, Ms. Lee. My former boss with Hunt Wesson and Denny's, recommended me to the company.

In October 1989, I started working for Taco Bell Corporation. Ms. Lee, the Director of Quality Assurance, was a tall confident, very direct, no-nonsense woman. She made the decision to hire me because of my interview. The Director of Operations was not happy with her decision because she hadn't gotten him involved. The corporate quality assurance manager was on vacation, so he did not have the opportunity to interview me either.

Learning from past experience, I knew I could negotiate the salary they made an offer. When they let me know the compensation, they were willing to pay me. It was more than I was making at Carnation's Pasta and Cheese. The job required me to travel, but they were not giving me a car, so I wanted compensation for my car's wear and tear. She respected my request and felt it was reasonable, so the offer included the additional compensation for one year. They accepted my counteroffer with additional compensation. Just like before, I let them know I had made a promise and couldn't start for a few more days. She agreed.

When my project with Mr. Larnard was completed, I started my career with Taco Bell. My knowledge expanded through my tenure with Taco Bell, and I really loved working for them.

Ms. Lee was a brilliant woman, and I knew we would work well together. I found out my position was new and would mainly work in the field, with my two counterparts already covering the two other regions. I had an office at the Corporate Headquarters in Irvine. I would be traveling a great deal of the time, which I welcomed.

I was in charge of all of the states west of Mississippi. I really liked the fieldwork, so I was excited about my new role. I didn't like sitting behind a desk. In the first few months, I would focus on the state of Washington.

Ms. Lee was straightforward, and after a while working for her, I learned that she had a good heart and really cared about her staff. Despite her stern demeanor and occasional swear word, immediately followed by a sincere apology, she was a very generous person. Every Christmas, she had a party at her home for those who worked for her. She took the time to go shopping for each of us. Not only did she give good gifts, but they were very personal. She also gave me birthday gifts, and they also were perfect for my interests. We all loved her parties. She has the same philosophy as mine "Work Hard and Play Hard"

Anytime you had a meeting with Ms. Lee, you had better be prepared. She had no time for long, drawn-out descriptions of the problem. She only cared about the solutions. She only wanted the bottom line.

Before working for Taco Bell, I researched the Corporation. It was started by Glen Bell in 1962, a pioneer in the Mexican fast-food industry! It then expanded as a national chain after PepsiCo Inc. purchased it in 1978. I was hired to work with regulators, to execute the food safety in the restaurants. I started with their food safety program for the managers and franchisees. My first task was to look at their food safety certification program geared for the restaurants. I studied the book and made sure I did well on the exam that the managers took. I wanted to have a thorough understanding of what they had been taught. I certainly didn't want to give a bad example. It was not written in a way that many of the restaurant managers and franchise owners would understand.

Taco Bell was set up differently from Denny's, because quick foodservice systems were very different from full menu sit down restaurants. They have different systems in place, and their product purchases were done in a certain way. It was one of PepsiCo's youngest restaurants. The others were Kentucky Fried Chicken and Pizza Hut. I had a lot to learn working in the field. To make sure I fully understood A to Z operations, I worked in the restaurant, making tacos, burritos, and the other items on the menu. Some of which were entirely foreign to me. I needed to experience all that happened in the restaurant, so I would have credibility in the field. It was only for a short time, less than a month, but I really learned a lot. It was exciting, challenging, and valuable learning experience. Later, I would be a part of a committee organized to update the food safety program, which was very important to the franchise owners and Corporate restaurant management.

After orientation, the next thing was to travel to Washington. My first priority was to build positive relationships with the food safety inspectors and the health departments. I was familiar with how they operated, having experienced them at Pasta and Cheese.

Government officials could be challenging to negotiate with. I had built a great rapport with the companies I had worked with previously, so I felt confident. Ms. Lee had shared with me that one of the reasons she hired me was because I had built favorable relationships with the inspectors in my previous positions. I learned you must set aside your ego when working with inspectors and government officials. This, with good negotiating skills and active listening, helped me a great deal. I had learned these things from my mentors, and my dad shared some of the same things with me. He never got into trouble, even though other Chinese businessmen in Indonesia went so far as to bribe the officials. I saw that my dad had good ethics and integrity. He never bribed them, as so many others did. With his gregarious personality and negotiation skills, he avoided any difficulties with them. To my dad, the consequences were too costly.

My father advised me, "Let them talk first, and really listen to what they have to say. It wasn't about who was right or wrong, just be interactive and remember it is all about solving the issue. Both parties are wanting the same outcome, it only makes sense to solve the problems in a way that was a win-win for both." I remembered the conversations with my dad, and it helped me anytime the inspectors came around.

My first goal was to meet with the Washington State Health Department's Director. He was aloof and uninterested in meeting with me. I explained to him, I was new, I wanted to be proactive and meet with him to solve problems through my persistence and sincerity, he finally agreed to meet with me.

The State Health Department was in Olympia, this is where I went to meet him. I had learned with government officials; it was better to meet on their turf. Especially if your corporate office is out of their area, you definitely want to go to them. I had to prepare myself for the meeting, and I needed to continually remind myself that anything he would say wasn't about me personally. My ego needed to be set aside.

Once he finished, I didn't try to defend it. I knew some things weren't true. But I kept my thoughts to myself. I simply asked, "What could I do to help you?" This threw him off guard. He had expected me to defend and argue, he was positioned to support his point of view, but I didn't bite. It took a lot of inner strength to hold my tongue, but I knew how powerful my words would be. I needed to play my cards right.

I let him know, I am new, I asked for him to give me a chance to get the issues corrected. I asked if we could have a fresh start. My intentions were to work diligently to fix the problems, and I had been given full responsibility and authority to do what was necessary to get the restaurants in compliance. Food safety would be my highest priority, and if his inspectors had any issues with Taco Bell, I was the person to contact. The only way to fix the problems was to know about them. I told him to call me anytime, and I will fly to any of the locations in Washington to meet and resolve the issues personally. He really didn't expect my responsiveness.

My position was to listen, don't debate, look to understand what he has to say until he finishes. He also apologized for his ramblings, he expressed incredible frustration to me, and I learned so much from the meeting. I was pleased that he understood my purpose and my strategy had worked. When I left the meeting, he knew I would do everything possible to resolve our issues. I had bridged the gap.

I learned it was necessary for building trust so we could work together effectively. I needed to be open and transparent. I basically told him our priority was food safely, and it helped him understand that we were striving for the same goal. And now, because I made the commitment, I knew I had to deliver.

Although the Director of the State Health Department as a whole had been reluctant, I watched his body language, it was telling me, I'll give you a chance. He was sizing me up. I'm sure he thought, We'll see if you do what you say you will do. I thanked him and told him, "All I want is to be given a chance to fix the problem in our field operations." He seemed pleased with my commitment.

After the meeting, I debriefed with Ms. Lee, and she was pleased with how it went. She gave me her complete support. She backed my stance, and she said the expenses were available to get the food safety in compliance.

Next, my plan was to meet with the King County Health Department. The State Health Department Director invited me to meet with all of the King County Health Department representatives. They were reluctant also. However, now I had the State's backing, so I met with them and started a relationship that helped me with the mission. I used the same strategy that had worked before and listened first.

I had made an impact as a Field QA Manager in the Pacific North-West. I knew we improved the relationship between Taco Bell and the government entities. I saw the proof of this relationship when I was invited to be a committee member of the Joint Food Safety Commission. The purpose was to bridge the government and foodservice organizations like Taco Bell. Ms. Lee was very proud of the work I had done and again was supportive of me being a part of the committee. She let me know I had a budget to be a part of the committee. I was also invited to go to their annual environmental health conference. I was also allowed to develop a relationship with the

Federal Food and Drug Administration and many local representatives in the affiliated government groups.

Now that Washington was well on its way to being where it needed to be, I now would focus my time and energy in the state of Oregon. If a company is not proactive and only reactive, it will have not have a good rapport with the stakeholders. In that case, you will not be able to get a foothold that would enable you to work together as a team if a crisis happens.

If a company is only focused on sales, they have missed the opportunity to be proactive and prepared for a crisis. It costs money to be proactive and build relationships having a liaison like my position. Fortunately for Taco Bell, Ms. Lee was a proponent of being proactive, and she saw in me the ability to carry out the master plan to bridge these relationships, which in turn improved the success of Taco Bell. A company must be proactive because it only takes one disaster to create a financial hardship and dearly cost the company. This has been seen with some foodservice manufacturing and packing companies. Not only did people get sick needlessly, and not only was there a financial hardship with the lawsuit payouts, but also in bad publicity.

When I was assigned, to solve food safety or regulatory issues, I had to go immediately. I found out most operators want to address food safety or regulatory issues and looked to me for answers. Most of them could have been very detrimental to the restaurants, but because they relied on my expertise and the relationships I had built, there was no food safety or media coverage. We were being proactive and able to manage it successfully. I learned before I traveled to the field I have to do my homework to be prepared for the assignment. I had to refresh my knowledge in microbiology from the microbiology courses I took at undergraduate and graduate school. I realize now if I had Google then, I could have learned so much faster. Gathering information was so much harder. We live in an amazing time with knowledge at our fingertips.

Because Taco Bell as a company wanted to be proactive in addressing food safety issues, our department decided to develop a crisis management policy and procedure programs. This way, the restaurant management had a consistent way to handle food safety crises across all states. Because each one of us came from different perspectives and had different strengths, we each gave valuable information on developing the protocols. The results were the Taco Bell Crisis Management program.

I enjoyed Taco Bell because they helped me grow professionally and personally. I made so many mistakes, but I learned from them. Sure, because of my personality, it is hard to admit some of them. They supported my growth, and I attended both professional development and personal development workshops. I took business writing, which was good for my professional development. It was a humbling experience. I had learned English as a second language. Still, the college courses didn't teach me how to write effectively in the business environment, which was very valuable during my time with Taco Bell.

Another skill set I acquired through workshops and conferences I attended was to be an effective trainer and make the subjects enjoyable. I taught food safety and learned how to teach to make it exciting and creative and not intimidate the students. It was essential to know the skills because food-borne illness could cause death in extreme cases without them. I learned to add humor in my teaching and not look so serious all the time! It was a humbling experience for me when I took a one week course on being an effective presenter! I realized I had done many things wrong, but that is what learning is about! I learned how the students would retain the information so they could apply it in their workplace.

As I made mistakes along the way, I know I learned from them. That was very important for my development, knowing that you should avoid future mistakes and this can change the way you do things. I think many people find it hard to make mistakes or are afraid of making mistakes. It is important to understand mistakes are a part of learning and growing.

In some work, environments penalize you for making mistakes. That in itself is a mistake. Businesses should have an environment that understands their employees need the freedom to take the risk of doing the wrong thing. When they have this attitude, they are far better off. I once thought if I made mistakes, it would affect my performance review. I didn't want to admit mistakes, or even to make them in the first place.

Did you know potato chips, Post-It Notes, and penicillin all were the result of mistakes? Our lives are forever changed by some of these inventions, which were first thought of as a mistake. As the decades have gone by and profits have been made, the benefit of mistakes has shown us again and again that failures were actually achievements. You've heard the old adage about Thomas Edison and the light bulb: When questioned on his many failures, he responded, he didn't fail 10,000 times, but succeeded in finding 10,000 methods that wouldn't work.

Sometimes we carry the childhood experiences into adulthood, thinking mistakes are bad. I realized there are many types of mistakes. Parents and teachers don't want us to make the same mistakes over and over again. Doing that means you aren't learning from your wrongdoing.

Through managing crises, I also learned some mistakes you cannot afford to make. They cost the company dearly, can be life-changing, and have severe consequences for your career. It is essential to follow through immediately with the task you said you would do. You can make statements that are taken out of context, and later on, you have to retract it. If you decide not to address an issue when you see it, because you were too tired or late at night or on the weekend, it could cause future ramifications.

You will avoid costly mistakes by learning from smaller mistakes. These usually show up to warn you along the way. If you ignore them, you may have to deal with a bigger issue later on. I am glad I decided to work for Taco Bell. Taco Bell invested in me, and I in them, making me a better employee and a better person. I have been able to take all of these skills and experiences along the way, and now I can help others through coaching because I use some of the same skill sets.

Life Lessons: your reflection

A thought to inspire you:

"If you plan on being anything less than you are capable of being, you will probably be unhappy all the days of your life." Abraham Maslow

What does this mean in your life? ....

....

....

....

Reflections to Empower you: ....

....

....

....

Have there been times in your life when you thought your mistakes were

bad? ....

....

....

....

What personality assessments have you taken, what insights about yourself

did you learn? ....

....

....

....

Have you discovered your blindspots, and developed ways to overcome them? ....

....

....

....

Reflections: what will you apply in your life? ....

....

....

....

....

....

....

....

....

....

....

"God's gift to us potential. Our gift to God is developing it."

Angeline Benjamin

CHAPTER 8

Relationships, Love, and Being Single

*"When you make a commitment, you create hope.
When you keep a commitment, you create trust."*
John Maxwell

My friend and coworker at Denny's wanted to celebrate my 35th birthday, and she took me to a place that I had never been before. She didn't tell me much about the place we were going to, I had no idea why I agreed to go. I supposed I wanted to celebrate my birthday and tried to have an open mind. Why not! It was my birthday after all.

This was a place for just women, as we walked in it seemed strange not to see any men. The only men were the ones that worked there, then I realized I was in for a new experience. Inside this place were male strippers who danced in an enticing way.

I was a very serious employee, and I thought for my birthday I should go to have some fun. I didn't talk to my fellow coworkers about my personal life, or activities outside of work, or my dates. In fact, I was dating but hadn't been serious about any of the men I had met.

On this night I thought, *I don't want to spend a lot of money so I'll just put my purse in the trunk of the car.* I remember clearly that I didn't grab my driver's license. It was still in my purse when we got to the door. The man at the door told me it was their policy to check identification before allowing anyone to enter. I was arguing with the man, telling him, "Hey you can tell I am over 21!" That was the age limit for the club. He went on to say, "Unless you are in your 50's lady we check everyone's ID!" I thought to myself, *I must look pretty good if they need to check my ID.* So I got my ID from the car so I could go in.

We got to our seats which were right in front of the stage. I didn't know it at the time but my friends, knowing how serious I was, had made bets on me.

They knew I liked to dance, but what they didn't know about me was that my competitive nature comes out when challenged. So they pooled their bets against me, they didn't think I would dance with any of the performers. There were about ten ladies in our group.

Back in the day, when I was in college, the guys were very shy, and wouldn't ask the girls to dance. Some of the girls were shy, and wouldn't ask the guys to dance. I was the exception, I would choose who to dance with. I thought if I am going to show up to dance, I was going to dance. I didn't bring dates to the dances in college, because I didn't want to be locked into dancing with only one guy. I always had this thought, *I didn't know these guys, it wasn't a big deal. I would never see them again.*

There was one performer that was very good looking and a very good dancer, so they bet I wouldn't ask him to dance with me. In the past, I asked guys to dance, and I don't ever remember anyone turning me down. I think they liked me because I was bold. Some of our friends had too much to drink, and put a lot of money in the pot, betting against me. So I whispered into his ear, "See all those ladies over there, well they are here with me because yesterday was my birthday. They brought me here to celebrate, and they have bet that I wouldn't have the nerve to ask you to dance with me. But if I do ask you to dance, and if you say 'yes,' I will get that pot of money from their bets. So, what do you have to lose, because if you say 'yes,' I will split the winnings with you?"

The guy looked at me and said, of course, I will dance with you. My friends were so shocked that I would do what I did, I was dancing with this hot guy, and they had no idea I had that kind of hutzpah! When the first dance was over, he asked me to dance again, we danced at least three dances, and even after the show was over, the man came back and asked me to dance again!

My friends were shocked, and said this was a side of you that we had no idea existed! I was not shy, and I liked to dance. I told them, I always say to myself, "Take action, what do I have to lose?" The women were all over him. At the end of the evening, the man told me he was honored to dance with me. I wasn't rude or pushy. He said, "I don't want your money, I said yes because I wanted to dance with you. I liked how you asked me with confidence."

The next day at work the ladies were so funny and told everyone about this other side of me that liked to have fun. That was the first time and the last time I went to this type of club. It was not a place that I enjoyed, drinking and spending money watching guys stripping. I was frugal when it came to spending money on entertainment.

I remembered when I turned 30 one of my goals was to save money to buy a condominium instead of continuing to rent an apartment. Three years later I was able to buy my own condominium - my own place!

After this experience, and turning 35, I thought to myself, I really like being independent. I spoke to my parents about still being single and they understood my independence, but they really wanted me to get serious and get married. All my sisters had gotten married and they thought it was time for me to find someone too. I told them I hadn't found anyone I liked enough to marry. My excuses were, I could travel anywhere I wanted, I didn't have to take anyone with me, and I could go anytime I wanted. I met many men and enjoyed their company for a while. At the end of the day, I would go back home, I go to work, and I liked the way things were.

Truth be told, I hadn't found anyone that respected me and that would accept me as I was. I was comfortable where I was at in life and found no need to change. Mary, the mom of one of my brother's friends, thought I might be a good match for her single friend. He was a young doctor and was Chinese. If I remember right, he was a dermatologist. In her mind, she thought I must be picky and waiting for the right man to come along. She thought I must be looking for an educated Asian man.

In college, I had dated some Indonesian men from other colleges, and we didn't get along because they expected me to be like other Chinese women they had met. They wanted the type of woman who would wait on them, and follow them around. That wasn't me. I thought that Asian men were male chauvinists.

So Mary told my brother about this guy and she set up a blind date with the young doctor for me. Typical me I thought, *Why not, one date couldn't hurt.* I didn't know much about him, but I did know he was educated in the States. My thought was he was a doctor, and maybe more sophisticated and less like other Asian men I had met.

He took me to a very nice restaurant, but the date was a complete disaster! He thought because I was Chinese I would be obedient to him and more like a traditional Chinese woman. As we exchanged conversation it was clear to me that there was no way this guy was for me. Again his attitude towards women was they should be home waiting on their husband.

At the end of the date, I told him, "I was very sorry, but our philosophies about wives were very different. I respected your views, but definitely did not share them. I was very open to meeting you, but I see you are like other Asian men I have dated that have expectations I don't agree with."

I later talked to Mary, she was shocked because she thought we would get along because as she said, "I thought you're looking for a Chinese man with a shared heritage."

After this experience, I realized the only thing I have in common with Asian men was a respect for our elders, family, and especially parents. I wanted a man that would respect everything about me, accept my family, my desires, ambition, dreams, and career.

For me I never went to bars to meet men, I didn't want a man that was a drinker, or would go out to drink and get drunk. I did talk to my parents again about all of this, they told me, "Angie, all we really want for you is to be happy." They could see I was happy traveling and working, and I always had good times.

I was content with my life. I would date guys, but they would want to be serious, get engaged, and married. I didn't believe in the tradition that at a certain age I should be married, and then have kids. I had never had a feeling that my biological clock was ticking!

I took an evening course at the local Junior college. It was a class about building relationships between men and women. Most of the people in the class were divorced or widowed. The people that were in attendance wanted to have better relationships the next time, more meaningful relationships. I learned a lot in this class. Relationships are more than falling in love and getting along with each other.

The instructor explained to have a better relationship there are two things to consider. One was to look for someone with an opposite personality than you, the instructor explained to me the psychology of this was so you don't compete with one another. For example, one likes to talk and the other is quieter. The goal is to enrich each other and grow together.

The students in the class disagreed, they thought that wouldn't work because it would cause disagreements. He said a dynamic relationship has a foundation on beliefs, and you can learn from each other when you are opposites. He told us, "Don't get mixed up between philosophy and beliefs or habits and personality." He gave an example, raising your kids, or finances. You can be an extrovert or an introvert, bold or shy, but your priorities, your philosophies need to match. The same personality doesn't grow, and after a while, the marriage will be dull.

Men and women naturally attract the opposite. He said, "Like my wife and I have opposite personalities, I like to be around people, and she likes to stay at home." He told me they argue sometimes. But our core beliefs, our finances, and how we raise kids we agree on. Respect is the foundation, he said. And your priorities need to be aligned."

If you are both introverts, you don't want to talk much, and you don't want to go out, you will always be inside, not doing things, no one is there to push the other to do things. It will be dull and eventually will lose interest in each other.

When it comes to relationships you need to know what things you value in the marriage. Some things will be negotiable and others are non-negotiable. It is important to sort these things out before you get involved in a serious relationship. Love sometimes blinds us to what we need and we compromise, then later we realize we are married to someone that does not respect the values we have. So these things need to be discussed at the during the beginning stages. If we never discussed them before marriage how would either of you know how you feel about the things you value and what things should be negotiated, and what is not negotiable? You can't change someone, too many people go into a marriage thinking, I'll get them to change because they love me. That may be in the beginning, but later on, it causes resentment.

Our instructor gave us homework, he said think about three to five values that are non-negotiable to you. Once you know what they are, share them with those you date. Ask your date to do the same. Determine the things that you would negotiate and the things you would never negotiate. Then don't sacrifice your non-negotiables.

Marriage is a contractual agreement, the more you know going into the marriage, the better chance you have of making it work. It is important to have this discussion before you fall in love. This was a completely new idea for me. I was equipped with the new information I needed. I knew this was an important part of why I was still single. I knew I needed to work on this, it was a point of awakening for me.

I sat down and discovered five non-negotiable areas that I knew I would not sacrifice in marriage. After a few dates, when it looked like things could be getting serious, I would have "the talk" about these things. I would let them know mine. They were usually shocked, just like I had been when I first learned about this in the class I took. But I wanted them to think about the values they would not compromise on so we could have an honest conversation about them and not after strong feelings develop. This was very important. I no longer questioned myself as to why I was single.

An Ideal Vacation

When I started my Taco Bell career, I was really enjoying the travel, and on vacation. My life was fulfilling. I found that my greatest joy was going on vacation and visiting my family.

One time my friend from work and I decided to take a trip together because we wanted to go to the same place. I didn't know her well at the time. My thoughts were it would be cheaper if we shared expenses and this might work better than traveling alone. One thing I didn't share with her when I am on vacation my life is not structured as it is at work. I like more of a spontaneous frame of mind, and I love to explore with no real set plans. I like to be adventuresome, and let the day take me wherever it wants. The only exceptions are when we commit to tours or events that are scheduled. I love having an open agenda.

We didn't discuss, and I didn't share with her how different I operate while vacationing. Because she only knew me at work she assumed I would be similar, having serious work habits like punctuality, and a lifestyle of being disciplined and serious.   We hadn't communicated ahead of time these differences or even the   preferences of what we like to do, and what we disliked.

What I like about vacationing is you have the freedom to do what you want, with no timeframes. We went to Club Med in Cancun. I thought they would have everything set up for us, with the freedom to do what you want.   I thought it would be a safe vacation also. Once we were there she wanted to know what time we would have our meals, and what time would we go to bed.   She wanted to know ahead of time what activities were going to do, but I didn't want to have a set plan, just go with the flow. I told her, "We are on vacation, just enjoy and do whatever you want to do."   She didn't understand that she could do what she wanted to do, and I would do what I wanted to do.   If we did the same things great, and if not that's okay too. That is why Club Med is a great way to vacation!   She didn't like how I presented the situation. There was friction between us and that's the last thing you want on vacation.   We didn't agree on what we wanted to do. I ignored her, and at the end of the vacation, it was clear to me that we were not a good match for travel buddies. What was worse than that was it ended our friendship and after that, we never talked again.

After that experience, I decided it was better to share a room with people I didn't know, that way there were no expectations.   Then I could feel free to do what I wanted and really have a good vacation without the hassle of trying to please someone who wanted a different experience than I did. I could sign up for a roommate, and I could be specific with the criteria that would give me the type of roommate I thought would be a good match for me.

I have always been money conscious, so sharing a room makes travel more affordable. After the experience with my coworker, I used a different way to save money and no longer had a problem with my travel roommates. I found traveling with girlfriends was not a great idea for me, because we have different interests, and especially not friends from work. It is better for me to go alone. If I meet a guy while I am on vacation, I can have a good time with no commitments to someone else.

When on vacation, I didn't check my email or voicemails. I just relaxed and I left the work behind. I always assigned my responsibilities to someone at work, so I could truly relax and have a good time with no agenda.   I even would leave the news behind with few exceptions.   I do remember the summer Princess Dianna was killed, I didn't know anything about it until I got home. I wanted to unplug, it was mentally energizing and relaxing.

While on vacation, I love to take photos, because I was alone, no one needed to know what I was doing. So my mindset was that of what happens in Vegas, states in Vegas. I felt as long as I stayed out of trouble, I could do what I wanted, with whomever I wanted, and I could enjoy myself. I wanted a total change of pace. Vacation helps you get away from the stress, it isn't life but a fantasy in some ways, exploring things, and having new experiences. At the end of the vacation, I'm mentally ready to get back to work. Often I would be exhausted, but after a good night's sleep, and I would be back in the groove.

My focus and priority was always my work, so my social life always took a back seat. The men I dated, they were not a priority to me. My parents never interfered with my life. Even at 40, they told me as long as I was happy with my life that was all that mattered, and they were proud of what I was doing.

Dating was good, but I made it clear I was not seriously looking for a spouse. I always dated professional men and intelligence was important for me when I did choose to go on a date. Maybe I just never found the right man, but this was how it was for me. I wanted someone with a steady job, ambition, and who was responsible. I did have a rule, never to date a married man, I never wanted the consequences. I never dated people at work. I didn't want to jeopardize my position.

Often when I dated men would want to take things to another level. I would normally break off the relationship because it would start to feel suffocated. My sister would tease me, that I had taken on the man's role in avoiding commitment. Some thought something was wrong with me, but I liked my freedom.

When dating, I felt it was important to communicate my non-negotiables, which was what I had gleaned from the course about relationships from years before. I didn't feel embarrassed, I was proud of how I felt and that I knew what I wanted. I also expected the men I dated to have an idea of the non-negotiable things they wanted in a relationship, and I would ask early in the course of dating. Once I discovered a man could not live with my non-negotiable list, I would cross them off my list and I wouldn't date them again.

I felt dating was about getting to know someone and what they valued if we were not a match I didn't want to waste my time.

Among those I dated, there were doctors, attorneys, engineers, entrepreneurs, and athletes. I had no desire to date performers, or actors, I liked people who had an opposite personality than I have. I stayed away from smoking, drinking excessively or recreational drugs. I didn't go to the clubs or bars to meet men, I just felt the men that hung out there didn't have my same values. I like men who don't talk a lot. I know I talk a lot, so when a man likes to talk it feels like competing. I don't like to compete in a conversation. These things are more important to me, much more so than their looks.

Older men typically want to control the woman in a relationship, so that doesn't work for me. I am in control of my life and I don't want someone else trying to control me. It was very rare for me to date someone older than myself, I dated men who were my age or younger. Because of Asian heritage, I may have looked younger than my actual age. Often men didn't realize I was older than they were. I truly enjoyed my home, living alone, and having time to myself. Many of my friends throughout my life had gotten divorced, often they inquired why I hadn't married when I was younger. I always explained, "It is better to be happily single, than miserable in a relationship," this is my philosophy.

During the dating years I would sometimes meet men that I liked, however, we didn't have chemistry, so we remained friends. Sometimes we had the same interests, and they even would set me up on dates that they thought I might like. Once my male friends would find someone and marry, I felt it was better for me to stay away. I would distance myself from them because I just didn't feel like it was healthy, and I would not want to be a problem in their relationship.

Being single was great because I never had obligations outside work. I go home when I want to, and if I wanted to stop at my parents' home, I could visit with them and have dinner. I enjoyed seeing them. I could eat when and where I wanted. Generally, Mami made extra, and I would take leftovers home to eat at a later time.

Because I traveled a lot, I met many men in other cities and countries. One time I met three married men who were on a bicycle vacation in New

Zealand. It seemed strange to me that they were vacationing without their wives. I wondered if they were separated or getting a divorce. They explained they loved their wives and they vacationed with them too and did many things together. They also said because they liked some vacations with their men friends and their wives didn't want to cycle or do what they wanted to do they had their separate vacations. They explained the men have men vacation, and the women had their women vacation doing the things they wanted to do together. They were professionals, one was an attorney, one was a dentist and one was an entrepreneur. They had all been friends for a long time and they trusted and respected their wives, and their wives trusted them. They were not like some men who look for women when their wives were not around. They were so much fun, they were wealthy and successful so they could take many vacations and had many great stories to talk about. I remember thinking at the time how wonderful that was. They also told me what they didn't like about women, like being needy, high maintenance, nagging, or if it was all about them. I liked getting to know them without the pretense of dating or other expectations.

When I was young and growing up in Indonesia, the expectation was for girls to marry and have kids at a young age. If a woman was not married by a certain age we thought there was something wrong with them. To me having kids was a responsibility with no expiration date. I was not willing to take on this responsibility unless I was ready for that commitment. Women shouldn't be ashamed of their priorities or make sacrifices if they decide to marry or not, or to have kids or not. I think we should marry freely. People who go into marriage expecting to get something from the marriage, rather than give freely with no expectation of something in return are going into it for the wrong motives.

Friends that I have talked to about this, especially women, have told me that they made sacrifices when they fell in love and married, and hoped they would get something in return. There later discovered they were disappointed when they were sacrificing and giving much more than they were getting out of the relationship. This is not the rule but a choice.

This was the case with my friend Gina. She had left her executive position rather quickly after meeting and falling in love with a man she met who was a wealthy physician. She thought because he was wealthy, she could retire, it wasn't what she really wanted at the time. By the time she realized she sacrificed for the wrong reasons, resentment came into the picture. She married and moved to a small town to give love a chance, however after a while she also discovered being in a small town had its challenges. All of the things she loved about living in Orange County, great shopping, nice restaurants, dancing, and a variety of entertainment options, and especially her family and friends, were not available to her in the small Midwest town where she had relocated with her new husband. All the money that she was provided didn't make up for the compromises she had made to marry him. They didn't take the place of the things she loved about living in Orange County, so they divorced. When you suppress the things you think you give up, but that you have passion for, they can't be replaced by love alone. You must have things in common, and you mustn't give up those things most important to you. The mistake I have seen people make is believing love is enough. I guess that is only in the movies!

Thinking about Gina and her marriage really made me realize the truth of the information I had learned years before in the class I had taken about relationships. Gina had followed her heart, but if she had known all of her values that were non-negotiable she would not have sacrificed the things she loved for a man that couldn't provide them. I learned from Gina, this valuable lesson. She loved the big city, not living in small towns. She found she was not cut out to be a housewife in a small town. She may not have known this until she tried however she did know she valued things not available in small towns.

Eventually, the things that may have seemed endearing at first no longer met her needs, and their marriage ended. After her father's death, she returned to California to run a successful family business that her dad had begun.

It is so important, to be honest with yourself, to develop a list of your nonnegotiable values. Then don't compromise; use your common sense to make your decisions. I believe that many women are not honest with themselves. We compromise on our non-negotiable, for the sake of love. If we do this, then when the honeymoon is over, the values we have will keep us in the relationship. It is important to be true to yourself, what you value, your passion, and not be ashamed if it isn't what is socially expected. There is no right or wrong.

When Mami married my dad, she freely gave up some things. She told me, "In my mind, I loved him very much. I accepted the way he was good or bad. I know I didn't want to change him in any way." Furthermore, she said,

"Sure some things about him I might not like, but I accepted him. The good was far above anything I didn't like." Dad was the same, he didn't expect mom to change, just accept each other the way they are. They had the same philosophy in life. They decided together, how to raise their family, how and where they wanted to live, and most of all they trust each other. I learned from my mom when you want to settle down, you must be able to trust and accept the other person. I was happy to be single until I found the man I decided to marry.

Life Lessons: your reflection

A thought to inspire you:

"Asking for what you want is a prerequisite for getting it." Alan Cohen

What does this mean in your life? ....

....

....

....

Reflections to Empower you:

Have you been in relationships hoping to change someone?
....

....

....

Do you have a non-negotiable list of the things you value? ....

Have you based decisions on following your heart? ....

....

....

....

How did it work out for you? ....

....

....

....

Reflections: what will you apply in yor life? ....

....

....

....

....

....

....

....

....

....

....

....

....

....

....

"If you believe in yourself,
you have the first secret of your success."

Angeline Benjamin

CHAPTER 9

My New Life

"The best and most beautiful things cannot be seen, nor touched...
But are felt in the heart."
Helen Keller

It was the day before our wedding, at the rehearsal I wanted to make sure everybody showed up on time. Even more importantly I wanted to make sure everything went smoothly. My sister, Indria, was the maid of honor, and my sisters, Josie and Bernadette were bridesmaids. Of course, my parents were both there. My husband Mike, his friend and best man Gabriel, and groomsmen Wendel and Johan were all in place. My nephew, Patrick, and my niece Melissa were both in the wedding party. As we went through the wedding ceremony rehearsal, I told all of them to follow the instructions, because the day was very important to me. My sister even remarked that I was being very bossy, somewhat joking, and smiling, she spoke with some truth. I have never looked at my personality as bossy, just that I know what I want and I communicate it so they know. Of course, they didn't want to disappoint me.

Later when I saw the video of our wedding day, I realized that my whole family, but especially my sisters and my brothers looked so serious, rather than excited when they walked down the ceremonial aisle. They followed through with everything that I asked them to do. My husband teased me by saying they look like they're walking into a funeral instead of a wedding. Then I looked at myself and I was happy and smiling at my guests. I did not look nervous. Why should I? It was one of my happiest days! My husband looked the most nervous.

Getting married for the first time at 48 years old I felt I am responsible for all of my expenses. I did not want my parents to spend the money to pay for the wedding because I didn't think it was appropriate. However, my dad and my mom insisted they wanted to help. They paid for dinner when my husband's family joined us at our favorite Chinese restaurant. We had a good time and we ordered some food that my father-in-law had never seen before and he did not want to eat it. It was okay with me but I thought it was very humorous. Everybody was very nice and polite. We had a good time. After checking different places, we decided to get married on a yacht. We decided not to have the wedding ceremony at the Catholic church (although we were Catholic), a long and unpleasant subject that I don't need to mention here.

Being a practical person, I had a budget for how much I was willing to spend on my wedding gown. So I went to Dave Bridal, a shop for wedding and party attire. I picked out my dress because it looked nice and practical. It wasn't a designer gown and the price met my budget! I told my sister, Indria, to coordinate with my sisters and my niece to find the dress they like. I did not want to get involved in choosing their dresses. I just told them the color, something in the purple family. I still have my wedding gown, I had it preserved just in case my nieces would want to wear it on their special day.

Mike and I decided to hire a wedding planner to make it simple, and because I didn't have a lot of time to plan the wedding. I preferred to rely on the experts! She gave us the choices for the flowers. I chose flowers that were in season and not expensive but my still my favorites. Mike didn't have an opinion so it was a quick decision. In fact, the person who helped us said that I was one of the fastest customers that she had ever had. For the cake, Mike and I decided together what we wanted.

On the day of the wedding, I insisted that get ready on my own. I told all my sisters and my brothers they're on their own too. I gave them the time to be ready and made arrangements to drive together to the yacht where the ceremony was held. We arrived early so we could take photos before the guests came in. My hairdresser fixed my hair, first thing in the morning, then I went to get my makeup done. We left for the yacht earlier than scheduled!

Certain things I know I did not go according to the plan. I learned to let them go, like everyone, I am a work in progress! For example, I assigned the wedding planner to make sure every guest signed the guest book. Perhaps I did not communicate with her clearly enough, because many of the guests who came to the wedding did not sign the guest book. What I think happened was no one was attending the book, or it wasn't in an easily accessible place. That's one thing about our wedding that I felt did not go smoothly. Everything else went very smoothly, well except the photos.

I didn't realize it at the time until I saw the photos taken by the professional photographer. My sister, Indria, was so busy trying to make sure that everything was going well when the photographer took our family photo outside, she was still inside and the photographer did not know. I was not paying attention either, after all, it was our wedding until I saw the photos. So that's why I did not have that photo framed. I was happy to have my entire family together.

The wedding was a special day, but what I cared most about was both my parents gave us their blessing. Even though my parents were devoted Catholics they were okay with us not getting married in the church. We chose to have the wedding during the day because we didn't want to have alcohol served at the wedding. Not only was it expensive, but also I didn't want to have a bunch of people getting drunk at our wedding.

It is nice to have a wedding on a yacht. All of the guests have to come on time and if they're late they miss the boat and the wedding. Because I had the wedding planner, she checked-in all the guests, so we didn't have any wedding crashers. My sister Indria, and Gabriel, gave memorable toasts.

We enjoyed dancing, and many of our guests participated. In fact, Mike's father and mother-in-law danced very well, everybody cheered them on. I got to dance with Papi, and that was one of the most memorable moments for me.

Although I hired a professional photographer and videographer, my two nieces took fun videos and photos, they are some of my favorites. Also, I put on each guest table a one-time-use camera, so we got a lot of fun photos. The food was great. The music was great. The only alcohol we served was when the best man and maid of honor toasted the two of us. Mike and I got to walk around and talk to our guests. All the guests were having a good time. My parents were very happy that I finally got married! I was the oldest daughter and I was the last one who got married!

That day, I remember, we had great weather. Not cold and not hot either, It was in the '70s. The yacht cruised around Newport Bay, in the early afternoon. We got back in the late afternoon, and it was perfect timing, so that was very nice. My brother-in-law let us borrow his classic Chrysler convertible and he drove us to my house. We had a family dinner at my house, read the cards, and opened the gifts. Then we went to the LAX airport, and traveled to our honeymoon in St. Lucia.

I'm a very organized person and my family and my boss told me the wedding was a reflection of my organization. My boss even told me this personally. I was the only one at our wedding that didn't look nervous, even when I walked down the aisle. One of the Taco Bell executives told me it was because of my training in managing crises. I laughed because I thought well maybe that's true. One of my goals was accomplished! I got married. No disaster happened! Everything went smoothly!

Non-Traditional Wife

What is a traditional wife? This is my interpretation. A traditional wife will often change their last name to their husband's last name That was considered normal at the time I was married. The children of that marriage also carry the husband's last name. This is almost expected.

My experience seeing many married, working women is that they often work in a demanding career and are also expected to take care of their needs and the household. I have always questioned this. Why is it that wives do all of these things, and husbands don't?

This was something I often discussed with my parents. Their response was always, "Well, that's the tradition." I challenge it, as I observed couples and families throughout my life, I decided I would not follow convention. It didn't seem like it was fair, nor did I want to live that way. If, and when I marry, this would be a subject of our conversation early in the dating relationship. I pointed out to my parents that they didn't follow Chinese tradition in their family decisions. Otherwise, they wouldn't have invested in the family's girls. My sister and I went to college, and because we were older, we went first. We agreed, traditions can progress. We were an equal opportunity family. Of course, this is not how most families with a Chinese heritage raise their family, especially in my generation.

When dating, I put into practice what I had learned many years before. If I saw the relationship had promise, the conversation of values and the list I had developed of my non-negotiables would be a conversation topic. I believe the discussion was essential and makes a good foundation in the relationship. Just the fact that you openly communicate your desires is more than many people do when dating. I knew if I found someone in agreement with me, I would want to get to know him more. I knew these things were what I needed to be happy in a marriage. If my date did not agree with my list, and I saw he was getting serious about me, I would break off with him. I know, even when you are in love, you might assume your spouse might accommodate your needs. At first, they would, but after a few years, the relationship would suffer if you both didn't have a full understanding of these things and agree with them. People can change, but they must want to. You can't change them with love. I realize that even with these conversations, there is no guarantee that the marriage will work.

I met Mike in a club for singles that focused on activities, not dating. The members are not pressured to date anyone. We got a chance to participate in bicycling, hiking trips, visiting museums, and other activities like these. After a few dates, before I developed deep feelings for him, I initiated the conversation about what was non-negotiable in my life as I had done many times before. I genuinely believe that I could not compromise on the non-negotiable values I established early on in my life. I knew I wanted to have these conversations before developing a serious relationship with the person I was dating. Mike agreed and understood. In fact, we talked about this later, and he said he really respected the conversation.

What were the things on my list? I needed a spouse that respected my career choice. My career was very important to me, and I let him know that I alone would choose when to work and when to retire. This was not negotiable for me. I would respect his career also. This is an example of what I call equal opportunity!

Another area we discussed was the acceptance of who I am. I needed my date, or future husband, to accept me just the way I am and not think he could change me somehow after we would marry. I knew we needed to value each other, accept, and respect each other in the relationship. He agreed because he would have the same expectation of me, and he was glad that I mentioned it and saw the importance.

My family's relationship is one of the top areas that I cannot negotiate in my life. If our relationship was going to progress, he would need to understand the importance of my relationship with my family and respect them. He also needed to understand, if they needed help, I would always help them. My siblings would also always be a part of my life. Even if he didn't necessarily like them, I wanted him to be respectful of them and respect their importance in my life. I learned throughout my life, not everyone gets along, but I hoped he would like them. Although he was in agreement with this, his family was not one of his non-negotiables. He didn't have a close relationship with his family.

Because I love dogs and have had them since childhood, I wanted dogs in our family. He agreed with this and felt the same way. So this was an agreed position for both of us. Things were looking good so far. He was happy that we both agreed on important aspects of a relationship. I was too!

There was another non-negotiable that I was firm about. I would not marry a man, or even date him if he smoked, drank alcohol excessively, or would take recreational drugs. I have seen the devastating effects of addiction in people's lives; I didn't want to have addictions in my relationships. I would not put up with that. He mentioned he did smoke in the past, but he knew it wasn't healthy and had stopped many years before meeting me. After the conversation, it looked good so far. We were off to a good start! Now could we get along?

Mike and I had similar philosophies in life, which is important. I look for that as well in relationships, because I didn't like feeling that I was in competition with the other person. And our personalities needed to complement one another. Mike and I have opposite personalities. Then we talked about the roles we would have once we were married.

We talked about kids, and if we would have kids or not, this was not a non-negotiable for either of us. We both knew we would need to adjust to our married life before considering adding kids to our family. My age was a factor, health risks were involved, it didn't seem to be an option. I didn't want to risk having kids myself. We would consider the opportunity to adopt if we made a decision at a later time.

We also talked about financial goals; this area of married life was not on my list of non-negotiables. It was not as important to me that he had a large savings account or financial portfolio. It was more important to me that he was educated and had a job of his choice.

More discussions would take place before getting married. He understood that I would not change my last name. Also, I would not be solely responsible for the housework, cooking, or laundry. These chores would be shared. He needed to understand that I might not want to cook every evening, and I didn't expect him to cook every evening. I knew I could cook when I wanted to cook but didn't have to cook, and it wasn't an expectation. If neither of us wanted to cook, we could get a take out dinner or go to a restaurant to eat. My career was demanding, and I knew I wouldn't cook every day.

As our relationship progressed, we decided to marry. So, on October 30, 1999, we made our commitment official and married. I just turned 48. As we entered into marriage, I was not a traditional wife. Having a husband was an adjustment, especially in the first few years. I had been very independent before the wedding. I sometimes went out with my friends after work, or exercised, rode my bicycle, and I wouldn't have dinner first. Then at times, I would go to my parents to eat dinner and visit with them. Mike's job had regular hours, and if I didn't go home after work, or if I worked late hours, he would be home waiting for me. I still traveled every other week most of the time. I needed to adjust my life, and I wanted to make it work. I knew it was my choice. I needed to look at my priorities. Mike had been married in the past, so he had experience with being married, and I had not. We both made adjustments.

Mike was not crazy about cooking but saw how much I worked and wanted to help. He decided he would make dinner for me when I was in town. I would give him a call before leaving for work. It was nice to have dinner waiting for me when I got home. The deal we made was that I would eat whatever he prepared. My mom also loved to cook, so sometimes we would go to my parents for dinner. During the week, my schedule was difficult to predict. But this seemed to work reasonably well.

Mike loved spending time with my parents. And although my non-negotiable values included Mike respecting my parents, he found that they were very lovable and easy to get along with, very approachable and understanding. He enjoyed spending time with them. As it turned out, he was closer to my parents than his own dad and step-mom. He loved it when my mom would ask him what he wanted for dinner, and she would prepare a special dinner for him. This really showed how much they cared for him. Mike being very handy, he could fix things around the house. So he always would make sure things around their home was in good working order. It was wonderful to see

Mike, who usually didn't talk much, sit with Dad, and talk for hours. You could tell they genuinely enjoyed each other's company.

Mike's mother had passed away from breast cancer years before I met him. Mike's dad was remarried, so we would call them each week, mostly on Sundays. Because family is so important to me, I wanted to have a good relationship with them; however, they lived in Virginia.

After we had been married for a few years, we decided we wanted to start another tradition, flying to Virginia to visit Mikes folks. They didn't live too far from Washington, DC, so we could explore many historical places and get to know them better at the same time. I really enjoyed spending quality time with them. Mike was pleasantly surprised when he saw how much his Dad cared for me. Being a very traditional man, Mike was not sure how his dad would react towards me. I was very independent and also because I didn't change my last name when we married. He thought his dad might not want to get to know me. As it turned out, it was never an issue. Mike's step-mom was also a very independent woman, especially when you consider those from her generation. We had many good conversations.

It's funny the stories we tell ourselves, and some of them we make them so much bigger, and often the issue never transpires. I got along well with Mike's dad and if he thought negatively towards me, it never showed. I learned from my parents when you respect people, they usually will give you respect in return.

It seemed like being a non-traditional wife was not a big deal. It is important just to be who you are. Being non-traditional was not an act of rebellion. It is who I am, and I embrace and feel good about who I am.

Life Lessons: your reflection

A thought to inspire you:

"Good decisions come from experience, experience comes from making good decisions." Mark Twain

What does this mean in your life? ....

....

....

....

Reflections to Empower you:

Do you have a "story" you are telling yourself, that may not be true? ....

....

....

....

Do you have strong convictions that you live by that are non-traditional? ......

....

....

....

How do you set boundaries for your convictions? ....

....

....

....

....

When have you asked for what you want in your relationships? ....

....

When have you been disappointed, and needed to just let it go to enjoy being in the present moment? ....

....

....

....

Reflections: what will you apply in your life? ....

....

....

....

....

....

....

....

....

....

....

"We don't choose our own family,
but friends are the family we choose for ourselves."

Angeline Benjamin

CHAPTER 10

Lessons From Our Dogs

*"I have found that when you are deeply troubled,
there are things you get from the silent devoted companionship of a dog
that you can get from no other source."*
Doris Day

My mom's early childhood experience caused her fear of dogs on into her adulthood. But Papi loved dogs and wanted them to be a part of his family. It wasn't until our neighbors moved back to Holland and they needed to find a good home for their dog Bear Tje, translated from Dutch it means "Little Bear." They already knew we loved her and felt our home would be good for her because we loved to play with, Bear Tje. She was an English Sheep Dog, maybe a mix and very friendly and loved to be with all of us. So, eventually, Eddy convinced mom to let us have our first dog.

Because of Bear Tje, my mom came to realize that not all dogs are mean, or would they bite and cause pain. Bear Tje was big but very gentle and she loved and protected all of us. She loved playing with us, and we loved playing with her. After years with Bear Tje she died of cancer. We were all so sad.

We were given a big German Shepherd by my parents' close friends when we were still in Indonesia, because they moved to the United States. We were happy to have her. Her name was Ang Tiong, which means in Chinese Mahjong, Red Dragon. She was also a gentle giant like Bear Tje had been. My mom was not afraid of her, because she was very gentle with her and all of us. Also, she was also a good protector for all of us. She never attacked anyone. I think because she was such a large dog, people who didn't know her were afraid to get too close to us or our home, which was very important to our parents.

There were many years that I wasn't able to own a pet because I was career-oriented. Because of this, when I married I knew this would be something I wanted very badly. So, Before Mike and I married we decided dogs would be a part of our married life because we both are dog lovers. As we considered all that we needed to know about the dog family we wanted to have, we considered many things. So we spent time looking at dogs, and we shopped for dogs, and after talking about it we decided we would get a puppy because neither Mike nor I had ever raised a puppy. We both had had young dogs and adult dogs but never a puppy.

We needed to know more about puppies, and how to raise one. We decided to go with a breeder that we found in a directory of dog breeders in a dog magazine. Shortly after, we put a deposit down on a male puppy from the litter of White Labrador Retrievers. We knew both the mother and the father of the litter. But we were not allowed to be near the puppies, because the puppies were only two weeks old and the mother was very protective. The father of the puppies was such a playful dog, he played with us. He was a big white, English Labrador Retriever.

Just before our wedding, we received a call from the breeder that the puppy we reserved had died. The mother had gotten sick and her milk infected the puppies. She gave us a choice to receive a deposit refund or she had another litter that we could pick from. We decided that when we returned from our honeymoon we would take the second choice and pick a puppy.

When we returned from our honeymoon we went to see the puppies, there were six altogether, four females, and two males. We had previously decided to get a male puppy. One of the male puppies was beautiful, he was calm and seemed to sit there and wait for us. He wasn't running around and jumping on us, or making any sounds, but calmly sat. The other male was skittish, he came to us but seemed timid. We decided to get the one that sat and look at us, calmly, and waited for us to interact. We discovered later by our dog trainer that this was the behavior of a confident puppy.

We brought the puppy home and named him Bruno, which was the name my dad suggested. Mike and I agreed with my dad's suggestion. We were very happy with our puppy. He was a wonderful little guy. He was independent and not needy, loyal, and was very easy to train. He was easy to please, and he wanted to please us.

Looking back, I really wanted to raise him correctly. I bought all kinds of books, there was not much information on the internet at the time. I read everything I could find about Labrador puppies. I became aware of all of the unwanted behaviors they warned about that you would want to correct as a puppy. What was funny, Bruno didn't have any of the things I thought I would need to correct. He was not destructive. I made sure I provided him the right toys, especially when he was teething. I put his toys in the freezer, he loved the soft toys with a squeaky sound.

He enjoyed his toys, and never destroyed anything in my house. I used pad training. I chose at that time not to crate train. I put the pads on the floor, and he knew exactly where to go when it was time for him to go. We put it close to the door so later on, we would move it, so he would go outside.

Bruno loved to go for a walk, like all dogs. So I trained him to walk on a leash. I also enrolled him in a training class. What I discovered was the class was not to train Bruno at all, but it was to train me on how to train Bruno. I found having the right instructor was very important.

At the park, Bruno was very obedient, even if there was another dog or any distraction, he stayed with me. We only used hand signs to control our dogs. We could not use voice commands. Bruno received the trophy for being the most obedient. We were amazed at Bruno's vocabulary, he understood many words.

There was another reason I thought Bruno was very special. We discovered his tongue was very thin and small by comparison to other dogs. Our breeder didn't know he was born this way. Although they said they would honor the guarantee and if we wanted they would give us a new dog. I looked at him incredulously and said, "No, that dog is our dog, we love him, we have him as is."

Even though Bruno had a non-functional tongue, and he learned to use the tongue he has, it was a challenge for him, but he learned to adapt. He didn't know he was different from other dogs. He was a wonderful dog and didn't let his lack of functional tongue stop him, he still drank his water and ate his food That is just the way he is. I also learned to adapt, I needed to learn how to give him a treat so he could take it with his mouth rather than like other dogs that would use their tongue.

From Bruno I learned, sometimes when people have a handicap, they don't want us to feel sorry for them, we should view them as able to adapt, this is something that is remarkable to us, but it is their norm.

We didn't want to crate Bruno when we were not at home, so we blocked off the kitchen. We wondered what he did all day when we were gone, so we got a video camera so we could watch him. I was amazed at what Bruno did all day. When I watched the recording, he entertained himself with his toy, then when he was bored or tired, he would go to rest in his crate. He used the pads when he needed, and was good being alone. He didn't cry or tear anything up, he played with his toy, and was very independent.

After some time, we thought maybe Bruno needed a playmate to keep him company. We were moving to a new place. When we got there we pursued another dog. We found a breeder in Long Beach, they were a very nice family who raised English Black Labradors. The breeder wanted to ensure our dog would be ok with introducing him to another dog into our home. So we brought Bruno to meet the puppies. He was so sweet and gentle with them. The breeder thought he was an unusual dog. I agreed, I thought I was blessed to have Bruno. The breeder recommended the male puppy. He was a Black Labrador, playful yet not aggressive at all. Bruno, met Bronson our new male black lab that day. We needed to wait until we moved to our new house before we could take him home. The breeder was nice and kept Bronson until we moved a week later.

Bronson was eight weeks old when we brought him to our house. He came in and went right to Bruno, just like they already knew each other. Bruno was about eight months old, and like a big brother to Bronson who followed Bruno everywhere. I didn't know about dogs doing this, but Bruno trained Bronson. I didn't need to go through house training the puppy, Bruno took care of that for me.

Bronson was very different from Bruno in destroying things. He destroyed many of Bruno's toys, and Bruno didn't get mad or anything. We were grateful that Bronson didn't destroy furniture or things that were not his, only the toys. One time he was bored, he chewed a hole in the wall. We needed to let him know that was not acceptable. We knew it was him because of the way he was acting, almost like he was ashamed of himself.

So I learned from both of the dogs, they had a friendship. They played together, they protected each other. They even cuddled with each other.

What I have learned from our dogs is they enjoy simple things in life. To me I think, people tend to make a big deal out of stuff when we should be enjoying the simple things in our life. All the dogs need is food and shelter, maybe a toy to play with and love. We give them plenty of that, in return, they show us, unconditional love. They have taught us to live in the moment.

Unfortunately, dogs don't live as long as humans. It is important to let you know how they passed away. We fed them well and took them to the veterinarian two times a year, or when they needed something. When Bruno was almost 11 years old, we found that he was vomiting blood. The doctor said something was wrong with his lungs. The doctor discovered he had lung cancer. I asked, "How long has he had this?" The doctor said it had not been too long, maybe only a few months. I wondered if I could have taken him earlier would he have been able to be treated. When we don't know, we can't beat ourselves up. We had noticed him having shortness of breath, but we thought he is getting old. We took him to a cancer specialist one week later because that was the earliest appointment we could get. In just a short time cancer had spread to his liver and kidney. The doctor explained to us that once this happens, it is really too late. He also told us that lung cancer is painful. On top of that, he had arthritis in both of his back legs, which we were able to control the pain by giving him supplements. We gave him pain medicine because I initially didn't agree with the doctor, I didn't want him to leave us.

Bruno seems to understand our feelings. He didn't eat much and had very little energy. It was like he knew his time was near, and I was not ready to let him go. He followed me everywhere and laid down next to me when I was at my desk working, watching TV, eating our meals, everywhere! He would look at me with his eyes that told me I am here for you. One of my friends who was also my vet mentioned that he was hanging on because of me. He felt it was his responsibility to be with me and to protect me. Once I learned this, I thought, *I didn't want him to live that way.* So one evening Mike and I had a talk with Bruno. We let him know he had done a good job, and he could go now. We hugged him, and whispered to him, he didn't need to hang on anymore. He seemed to understand, then, he fell asleep, looked very peaceful, we all on the floor.

The next morning he was not able to go outside by himself anymore. Mike took him outside but he wasn't able to relieve himself. Once back inside he rested on Mike's lap, he seemed to be at peace, he seemed so calm. He wasn't trying to follow me, or protect me any longer. A few minutes after that he passed away.

We were so sad for many days, but we knew he was not suffering anymore. Bronson seemed to miss him also. I reflected on life with Bruno and the end of his life. I learned maybe I had been keeping Bruno alive for me. Sometimes we forget that when dogs suffering it is unlike people. Dogs are devoted to us, and when they are not able to give any longer they have no purpose any longer.

Bronson was sad that Bruno was gone. He didn't want to play, or eat. The doctor checked on him. Although he had a kidney problem, he was okay but missing Bruno. We were living in New Mexico then, and we decided to adopt another puppy a rescue puppy from the dog kennel. Mike and I fell in love with this cute female black Labrador-Rottweiler mix. The mail carrier found her in the Walmart parking lot. We decided to name her Lucky. We brought Bronson to meet Lucky. It was so amazing to see him came alive. He had a new purpose. His new job was to train Lucky. Mike and I couldn't believe the difference in Bronson.

About a year later Bronson's kidney was failing, and he couldn't eat, he did not sleep well. We knew we didn't want to have him suffer as Bruno had suffered. We talked to him, and he seemed at peace, he was in tune with that. So we chose to put him to sleep, in a more peaceful way. It was so hard to say goodbye to our dogs. I didn't want to keep Bronson alive for my sake, it was not fair for him to suffer.

Why did I want to tell you this story? Our life has a purpose, Bruno and Bronson made that so evident to me. They taught me not to complain and to live my life with meaning. If you can live in a way that helps others and share what our dogs have taught us we will be a lot happier. They were so happy, they wanted to please us, they showed us how much they loved us every time we returned home after we take them for a walk and fed them. Bruno taught me not to let any physical handicap or any challenges stand in the way of fulfilling your purpose or prevent you from the achievements you want in your life.

Life Lessons:

Reflections to Inspire You:

"I think dogs are the most amazing creatures; they give unconditional love. For me, they are the role model for being alive." Gilda Radner

What does this mean in your life? ....

....

....

....

Reflections to Empower you:

Do you have a childhood experience that could be holding you back from something good in your life now? ....

....

....

....

Have you had a pet that taught you a life lesson? ....

....

....

....

Has someone, even a pet, helped you feel unconditional love? ....

....

....

....

Reflections: what will you apply in your life?

"Dogs greet you with enthusiasm
whether you've been gone for one hour or one year."

Angeline Benjamin

CHAPTER 11

Learning To Balance Life

*"You need not feel guilty about being able to keep your life perfectly balanced.
Juggling everything is difficult.
All you really need to do is catch it before it hits the floor!"*
Carol Bartz

During my early years working at Taco Bell, one of my responsibilities as the Quality Assurance Manager was to perform food safety and quality audits. In this job, I needed to enforce compliance regulations and laws. If the restaurant was out of compliance then a consequence was applied.   This was the same as the health department, only if it was severe non-compliance the health department would close the restaurant until the infraction was corrected and reinspected.

When I came to Taco Bell, I learned about their operation and how non-compliance issues would affect the franchisee and corporate-owned restaurants.   If a restaurant was out of compliance, we would develop an action plan, and a consequence was applied.   The same philosophy applied to the state and federal health departments and the FDA inspectors.

After some time working to achieve compliance, I realized there was more than just compliance. It was more to be proactive, and to prevent serious food safety issues from occurring in the restaurant. Most of the people at the restaurants were intimidated by me.   And rather than have me help educate them, they would hide problems, hoping I wouldn't find out. However, I needed to know their operation.   This way I could help them so their restaurant wouldn't be shut down by one of the health agencies, or worse yet, have a food borne illness that affects many patrons.

Most of the employees wanted to do what was necessary to keep their restaurants in compliance with the policies and the laws.   Very few didn't care.   No one in the right mind goes to work and thinks who can I get sick today.   Or worse yet, who can I kill today with bad food. They don't have these things in mind. Most don't know and don't understand why they must do things to keep the food safe. Educating the people at the restaurants was very important, and so they would know why they should do what is asked of them.

Back at this time in my life, it wasn't easy to admit I needed to change my approach at work. I took my job so seriously, and my mindset was to have my area of responsibility in compliance. I found most people had many things on their minds other than compliance. So I needed to understand this and shift my mindset so I could be a better influence on them. I appreciate the upper management of Taco Bell for investing in my training and showing me the importance of personal growth by sending me to workshops.

My favorite workshop was one that I learned how to change peoples' perceptions when I was teaching a workshop. In another class I learned negotiation techniques. There are some people who get stuck in the way they do things and the way they were educated, and they are resistant to change. I could understand this. When it comes to food safety it is black and white! That is why certain protocols must be followed.

When I visited a restaurant, I was an outsider. And to make matters worse, I was telling them how to do things. It would be like your Mother-In-law visiting your home and telling you how to clean house, or worse yet rearranging your kitchen. They could have been doing things in a certain way for years, however, it could jeopardize food safety. I understood how difficult it was, but my job was to ensure compliance. You must look at the risks and benefits, and also the grey areas. Most laws are in place to protect the consumer. However, there are more things to consider than just the laws. Some areas that are important might not be in a written format, these are the grey areas that need to be considered.

Eight years later, in late 1997, after Yum Brands became the parent company of Taco Bell, Pizza Hut, KFC, and Long John Silvers, I was given the opportunity to be the Food Safety Officer for the entire Taco Bell Corporation. So I no longer worked from home except occasionally to catch up. In order for me to fully understand the entire operation, I needed to be at the corporate office. So although I could work at home, I felt it was better for me to go into the corporate offices. It was my decision to make, as I still had the latitude to decide what was best for me to get my job done. We all felt I could be more effective to have an office in the corporate building.

One reason for me to be in the corporate office, it was important for me to get to be visible and know all of the department heads. They needed to know I was a part of the team and I was approachable and wanted to be involved. Marketing, menu development, product development, supplier compliance, all of the departments would have interactions with me, and together we would ensure the same objectives.

Nothing happens overnight, but I did see changes within all of the departments especially menu development and product development as they began to see me as a resource rather than a hindrance. They needed my approval, so it was important we work cooperatively. Previously, I would just say, "No you can't do it this way." Over time, I changed my strategy. Each time they would come to me, I would simply ask, "What are you proposing?" I didn't want to do their work. I gave them examples and options and educated them on the interpretation of the food codes to have a fuller understanding.

For example, to destroy bacteria in foods it must be heated to and reach 165 degrees. You can't change the food safety laws. If it is only heated to 160 degrees, that is not okay and is out of compliance. If an inspector were to observe this being done we would be subject to an infraction as a critical violation. The way food handled could vary, but the end result couldn't. So, I needed to know what they were doing, but to help them, I would ask them good coaching questions like, "If you were in my position, what would you do?" I wanted them to think, rather than just having me telling them the answers. They would need to explain their process. First, we would talk about the absolutes of food safety laws. Then I would look at their process to ensure the end result was a product that was safe.

The people I worked within the restaurants were more open when they saw me as someone that could help them, educate them, and not just someone who brought consequences. To create this relationship, I would engage them in a conversation and would ask them questions. By doing that, they could explain their process, and they were more open to the discussion, and additional questions.

What was most helpful, the Taco Bell organization took a stand and made the message clear. From the president and all throughout the corporation, including the franchisees; do not compromise food safety. This was a non-negotiable, everyone needed to understand the risks and benefits of compromising food safety. The law and how it is enforced may be subject to interpretation. I learned this from the FDA inspectors, officers, and the Director of the Health Department. The number one objective was always the same, the safety of the customers and the employees. We did not want anyone to get sick with food-borne illness or communicable disease. The only way to carry out this objective is to carefully follow the food safety guidelines.

Another big push throughout the corporation was food safety crisis management. We learned from the past, there were ways to effectively handle a food safety crisis. Collaboration is very important when developing systems and policies that involve how the food safety laws are carried out.

When there is a crisis, there is no collaboration. It was important for everyone to understand the entire process by educating all parties in the company who were involved in the program, including the representation from franchisees. It is very important the management from the top have buy-in and accept the Crisis Management Program. We must be proactive in our approach. At the end of the day, the program was a success because everyone saw the results, the procedures were being followed, we had fewer incidents, and fewer negative media exposures. Through this, we gained the respect of government officials.

The Crisis Management Program spread throughout the Yum Brand organization which also included Kentucky Fried Chicken, Pizza Hut, and Long John Silvers. All of the quality assurance professionals worked together to ensure the program was being carried out efficiently. In fact, there is a Yum Brands Food Safety and Regulatory team that supports all brands when it comes to food safety and regulatory issues. I was very proud of my involvement as I was given the responsibility of leading this program at Taco Bell. I believe I was given this responsibility because I was not afraid to make decisions, and the management saw my leadership qualities. I believe if you are given responsibility for something, you need to look at all of the data, then make a decision. In a crisis, there can be no indecision. There will always be a crisis', what is important, how you manage it. You need to know the plan of action based on previous issues. Some decisions are made well before a crisis happens. You stick with the facts, not emotions or personal opinions.

Learning a way to approach people about food safety, as a coach rather than an enforcer, gave me a passion to coach people. I needed to change my attitude, my body language, and approach people in a way they can trust me to educate them in an interactive way that helps them want to comply.

The franchise owners needed to know I was approachable, but also could show them I could be firm when I needed to be. Mostly they needed to know I could be trusted, I was on their team! My goal was for them to understand that I was there to ensure they stay in business. I tried to put myself in their position so I could see both sides of the issues.

One of the most insightful opportunities I had was when I was invited to the franchisees' annual meeting to listen and learn from them. The group was asked if they knew who I was, and most of them did. They were also asked if they feared me. Again most of the franchise owners agreed, they did fear me. However, when they were asked one final question, which was, "If you were in a food safety crisis would you welcome Angeline to help you?' They all unanimously agreed. I was surprised but learned I needed to find a way to approach people in a way that I didn't intimidate them.

One thing that would have helped me back then if I was able to know and accept myself. I would have been aware of my personality and acknowledge and own it. Being aware of my blind spots would have helped me also. I knew I was an extrovert, with a logical mind and I made my decision mostly from facts/data rather than using my intuition. Then I could have grown and learned how to interact with people in a way that was not intimidating. I had developed a rapport with some of the franchise owners because I had helped them in the past. They were so helpful when I asked them what I could change. I didn't want them to fear me, I wanted to be welcomed because I could help them.

One other method I used to get buy-in from franchise owners who were resistance to the food safety program, or to me. I met with other franchise owners that could be a third party that spoke on my behalf. By doing that we were proactive, and all of the crises that occurred during my tenure were handled without guesswork. They were trained, knowledgeable, and knew the procedures to follow. I was very proud to be a part of the Taco Bell team. We all know incidents of food safety is not a matter of if it happens, but when it happens. It is so important to be prepared, it is so much easier and manageable when you are. This is two-fold, a procedure needs to be in place and they need to know how to execute the procedure.

During this time I was passionate about my work, I was driven to make sure everything was in place. I worked long hours, I traveled in the field and loved what I did.

My family suffered

Years later, when I reflected back on that time in my life, I realized my time with my family suffered. You can't get the time back. My parents never complained or asked me to give up working so hard to spend time with them. They never make me feel guilty for putting so much of myself into my work. They never said anything about the vacation together that I had promised them so many times. They were supportive and understanding and took a back seat to my work.

My husband also put up with my long work hours, he had agreed that my work was very important to me, even before our marriage. But at times I know he wanted to spend more time with me. I could tell, not by what he said, but what he didn't say and his body language. My excuse was, that is just the way I am.

After my siblings and I reached the age when we did not take vacations with our parents anymore, they did not go on long expensive trips outside the country. They had saved all of their money to give us the opportunities to be educated and be in a country where we could succeed. This was their sacrifice, and without it, we wouldn't have had the opportunities we had experienced. My siblings and I decided to send our parents on an annual vacation out of the love and sacrifice that they had made for us. We sent them to Europe to experience the pilgrimage in France and Spain, and to go to the Louvre. This was impactful because they were devoted Catholics. Another time I sent them to Hawaii on their own, just the two of them. I thought, at the time, it was what they would have wanted. But what they really wanted was for us to have experiences with them.

One of their favorite trips was when we sent them to China. It was a trip of a lifetime for them. They told me it was one of the best trips they ever had because of our heritage and the places they had longed to see. It was a very emotional trip for them. When they returned they told us they wanted to go again but next time they wanted us to go with them.

Although I worked long hours and was very devoted to my job, having vacations were very important to me. I never lost my vacation time because I didn't take it. I would calculate how much time I had, and figure out when and where I would go way in advance. I knew I needed this to balance my life. In my opinion, this was a reward the company gave us as a benefit. Therefore I would always use it. After Mike and I married, we would take vacations together.

One thing I really wanted to do was to take my parents on a cruise because they talked about it at length and they thought it will be fun. Mike had decided not to go, he didn't like the idea of going on a cruise because he suffers from seasickness. He wanted me to go with them so I could focus on enjoying my time with them. So I thought, *Let's go to the Mexican Riviera.* I got a nice suite for us. I had learned in the past when you travel it is important to have travel insurance, just in case something comes up. Especially with older people you never know if something might happen.

My parents were so excited to go on the cruise with me. About two weeks before we were scheduled to go, my dad called and told me his skin was itching. We thought maybe it was the excitement, or anxiety, maybe even allergies.   The doctor prescribed an antihistamine, but it didn't help his condition. When I went to see him, I saw that his eyes looked yellow and knew it was jaundice.

Years before my dad had contracted Hepatitis C after having surgery in Indonesia.   He had a gall stone removed in the 1960s, he had needed a blood transfusion at that time.   The practice then, people would sell their blood for money, and there was no testing for communicable diseases. Afterward, they discovered my dad had Hepatitis C, they gave him medication. It made him very sick, and the doctor told us just to watch his symptoms because it seemed to be in a dormant phase and could be that way for a long time.

In the early 2000s, Hepatitis C was still somewhat rare in the general public. We knew to watch out for the symptoms just in case it might become active. It can stay dormant for years, then suddenly flare-up, so he had an annual exam to watch for this.

Learning about communicable diseases caused by bacteria, viruses and parasites was a part of my job. Anything that can be transferred to people through food and poor personal hygiene, direct contact, sexual contact, etc. So I kept up to date on all of the communicable diseases including Hepatitis C.

I urged my dad to be seen again and when he arrived at the doctor's office he passed out. It was very serious and he was hospitalized. The doctor let us know that the Hepatitis-C Virus had spread, and was invading his organs especially his liver.

This was a shock to all of us. It had just been a few months since he had been tested and the doctor had said the virus still dormant. He did manage high cholesterol and high blood pressure but had no other health concerns. Sometime between May and when he got sick in December of the same year, the hepatitis C virus activated and started to spread. We went to see a gastroenterologist, a specialist that specifically treats patients with Hepatitis C. He told us that our dad had cancer of the liver.

My parents would always take one of us to their medical exams. They wanted to make sure they fully understood clearly, even though they understood English very well. They trusted us, and always wanted us to know about their health. Our parents had their plans in place with a medical directive and also a will. They wanted me and my siblings to make medical decisions if they could not. My family trusted me to go with my parents and to listen to the doctors, advocate for my parents, and support their decisions.

My parents had made it very clear they didn't want to be on life support, and if they were going to pass away they wanted to be at home. They also bought their burial plans so no one would need to make arrangements after they passed away when it would be emotionally difficult and stressful. Because they were Catholic, they had made the decision that they wanted to be buried, and they had everything set up and paid.

We then went to see an oncologist, who explained to us cancer had spread and was in his bloodstream. She let us know there was nothing she could do and my dad should enjoy the time he had left. I will never forget the look on his face and the face of all my siblings. The doctor said it would be her best guess that he only had one month or less to live. He was 79 at that time. I watched my father as he processed the news. He told us, he had done all he could do to be a good father to us, and he hoped we knew that. We canceled our vacation.

The Unexpected Loss of My Parents

After the appointment with the doctor, we returned to my parents' home. Dad seemed to have taken the news well, but he said he just wanted to be alone for a while. We all understood, but it was a really hard day. We had been so excited to go on a cruise just the week before. It was a lot to digest.

My dad asked all of us to stay with him until he passed away. He asked us individually if he had been a good father. It seemed like a strange question to me, it had been obvious to each of us that he had been a wonderful father. We couldn't believe he would even question it. He had provided for us, he had loved us, he made sacrifices for us. I thought maybe he was asking just because he was facing the end of his life. Parents try so hard to be good to their children. My dad didn't have parents who were good role models, maybe he needed to have the acknowledgment from us that he had been a good father. After that, he had a private talk with my mom, and he seemed content.

We were warned about the progression that would happen as cancer would continue to spread. We told him he could eat anything, do anything, but he had no appetite. The hospice nurse came to provide support for us. We were told he would have a build-up of ammonia in his bloodstream, that cancer would get to his brain, and that would cause him to go unconscious. We thought we had more time, but only a few days later he slipped into unconsciousness. The hospice nurse administered a small amount of morphine to keep him out of pain. We knew the time was close. My brothers wanted to care for him to ensure he was clean.

It was early in the morning he woke up, spoke to each of us, and then passed away. It was so hard for all of us. I reminded everyone that we should be grateful because he passed so peacefully and he did not suffer a long time. I reminded them about my friend's dad who had passed away from liver cancer and had been in great pain and suffering for months before passing away. Dad didn't suffer, he had the Last Sacraments, and then God called him home. He had been at peace. Of course, we would have wanted him to stay, but it would have been selfish to keep him. God made the decision.

My youngest brother took it the hardest because they were living with him. He somehow thought it was his fault, I assured him that was not. One of their neighbors, who was a very religious person and a nurse, told me that God must not have wanted him to suffer because dad was a very kind person.

I knew my mom loved my dad so much. My parents had a very good marriage and rarely had arguments. As I learned from my own marriage, arguments sometimes are healthy in a relationship. We all are human, we can't be in agreement all the time, but as long as there is no violence, hatred toward each other, and each is able to respect each other's deferences. In my opinion, this is part of growing old together. They kept their disagreements to themselves. They would tell us arguments are okay, they help you express the things you have inside. It is important not to keep them bottled up.

Mom was one of the most forgiving people I have ever known. She would say you must forgive, if you don't, you are no better than the other person. It isn't always easy, and we don't need to forget. She would give people a second chance. After dad passed away she really suffered from a broken heart. She had no interest in life. She didn't believe in suicide, so she would never do harm to herself. She had just lost interest. A few months went by, and we all wanted to celebrate her birthday with her.

So we kind of tricked her into going on a cruise to celebrate "Papi." We went on a short Mexican Riviera cruise, for a few days. She really had a good time, she was happy. She was happy because we all went with her to celebrate. She even danced and I have a picture of her that I still treasure.

After the cruise, we talked about going to Rome, Italy. However, she would put it off. She would prefer to go shopping with me now and then, but the conversation was always about Papi, I knew she really missed him.

She had a routine doctors visit a few months later and the doctor advised us that her heart was getting weaker and weaker. She was also asthmatic. The doctor gave her medication for her heart, but she told him that she didn't want to take any more medication. When he questioned her, she said she wanted to join her husband. The family doctor understood her wishes. Mom just wanted to be left alone. The family doctor knew it was her way of saying goodbye. She impressed upon us that we always need to forgive and support each other. We might have an argument, but never leave it unforgiven. One afternoon my mom called the priest from their church asking for the Last Sacraments.

The following day she had told us she was tired and wanted to take a nap, but she wanted to talk to us first. She thanked us and we all knew she was saying good-bye. I knew not to argue, she was at peace. While she was napping we all sat around her, she passed away in her sleep. The nurse who was her neighbor verified her heart had stopped. As mom requested, she did not want to be resuscitated and she wanted to pass away at home. So we granted her wish. Mom told us her job was complete, as a mom and a grandmother. We all had people to care for each other. You need to honor your loved ones, their wishes. Our parents asked us to live our life the fullest, with no regrets, and we knew we were loved by them.

One o the beautiful gifts my parents provided us was their final burial and memorial service which was completely planned and paid years before. Mom was at peace with her long time love who had been waiting for her.

Losing my parents caused me to rethink things. Mike had talked about owning his own business for some time, but my excuse was I didn't want to leave my parents. So now, I didn't need to stay in California for them. If we were going to do it, we needed to do it before we were too old and would regret it later. I didn't want Mike to be sitting on the front porch retired one day with the regret of never giving entrepreneurship a try. I wanted to support him, and go for it.

Mike had put up with my crazy work and travel schedule during the six years we had been married. I felt like it was his turn to do what he wanted. We had two years of savings, so he was able to work on setting up all of the aspects of the packaging business he had visioned. This way he could use his unique talent as a packaging engineer, and I could start a consulting business to help other corporations set up their food safety programs.

Five years before, I had discovered I was qualified to retire and collect my pension when I turned 55. I was hired when Taco Bell still provided pensions, for which I was grateful. Their policy on retirement had changed a few years after I had been hired, to a matched 401K plan. I banked as much as allowable into a retirement account and they matched the funds.   So for every dollar, I put in they put in a dollar. It was a really good deal. I invested as much as I could, to supplement my pension.

After having a meeting with my financial advisor at the bank, I learned about the Taco Bell pension funds guarantee policy. I decided to cash my pension in a lump sum, then I could invest 60% into my retirement account and 40% to start our businesses. This coupled with our savings account gave us a safety net for the next two years, just in case my consulting business and Mike's packaging business didn't grow. We didn't need business loans.

We built a new custom home with a larger lot, it cost 60% of the value of our home in California. We loved the one-story floor plan and almost an acre of land. Because of that, we made a decision not to sell the house in California and we made it a rental property. We hired a property manager so we needn't worry about it. Mike moved to New Mexico in November to check the progress of the home and started his business plan. The builder told us, we could move in by the first week of January 2007. I gave notice to Taco Bell the day I turned 55 and retired the day following my birthday in October 2006. When I gave notice, I told them if they were not able to fill my position by then, I could work temporarily from New Mexico. Everybody was surprised that I was retiring at my age, so I assured them it has nothing to do with the job. It was time for a new chapter in our lives and Mike wanted to open his own business.

In January 2007 I moved to New Mexico, we were surprised that the winter was one of the coldest that they had in ten years. It was going to take a few more months for Mike to open his business, I continued to work for Taco Bell, managing from New Mexico. I would fly to the corporate offices once a month. I figured, Taco Bell eventually would hire someone to replace me. Meanwhile, the head of quality assurance wanted to hire me as a consultant for at least a year until the new person they planned to hire settled in. Then, we found out, they couldn't hire me as a consultant, because of the terms of my pension. Since I did not want to lose my pension, I wasn't able to do any consultant work for them. I still could be a consultant to other corporations. I officially retired in May 2007 and started my consulting business in the same month. I had a client already waiting for me to help them. Mike opened his business, Pack N' Ship in July of 2007.

Life Lessons: your reflection

A thought to inspire you:

"Forgiveness is the key to action and freedom." Hanna Arendt

What does this mean in your life? ....

....

....

Reflections to Empower you:

Do you need to take time to have experiences with your loved ones?
....

....

....

....

Have you planned for retirement? ....

Have you received feedback that you didn't like but it was what you needed

to hear? ....

....

....

....

Are you making excuses in your life that you do things because "That's just

the way I am?" ....

....

....

Reflections: what will you apply in your life? ....

....

....

....

....

....

....

....

....

....

....

....

....

....

"Spend time with those you love because one of these days you will either say, 'I wish I had,' or 'I'm glad I did.'"

Angeline Benjamin

CHAPTER 12

My Experience As An Entrepreneur

"People have a remote control in their heads today.
If you don't catch their interest, they just click you off."
Myrna Marofsky

In July of 2007, we opened a retail store called, AM Pack N' Ship, a packaging business in Albuquerque, New Mexico. Mike did research on the best way to open the business and because we were new to the business, Mike bought a license and a brick and mortar, physical business. It included a business model and a starter package including the basic equipment, furniture, and products he needed to open the store. Once we opened the business we received support for a year on how to run the store, with coaching for a period of one year. This gave it a starting point to obtain all of the supplies he needed and it was the foundation for expanding in the future.

Santa Fe, New Mexico is a world-known art center. Our business catered to the arts, and Mike was able to provide packaging for art dealers. His plan was to expand to industrial packaging, where the profit margin is higher and he has a lot of experience in that field. There were great Native American art and artifacts in the area. Some of the pieces were fragile and this took packaging expertise to ensure safe shipping. That is where Mike saw the potential to use his expertise. My part of the business was to support him and look for potential clients through business networking. The business started off really well for a new company, however, in the fall of that same year, the economy was not as favorable.

Fortunately, when I retired from Taco Bell, I was able to acquire two mid-size companies as consulting clients for food safety systems. I was willing to travel to their California Corporate offices and Washington State. This was very fortunate, and the consultant contracts helped us while getting the packaging business established.

As the economy worsened, I eventually lost the contracts with the two corporations as they reprioritized their funding. I looked for businesses in the local area that might need a consultant. Mostly they didn't understand the value of hiring a food safety consultant, especially in the economic climate of 2008. I conducted a food safety webinar, hoping to attract consulting clients. It was promoted on a training site and I got residual royalties every time the product was sold, I owned the intellectual property. Once a month I did online training about food safety and crisis management. I would emphasize the importance of having a coach in the business. It had topics like what to do about employee illness, and food-born illnesses, communicable diseases, and also what to do in case of a product recall.

In times like these, which we are sure to experience again, the economic crisis caused problems and seemed hopeless. During these times create opportunities for yourself in the business world by reaching out to others and utilizing your skills to fill a need and continue to reach the goals when in an economic downfall.

We developed relationships with some of the lower end art businesses that sold Native American art. We got to know the business owners and learn about their Native American heritage and culture. We were invited to some of their celebrations and the Pueblo culture is something you can see all throughout New Mexico. They were not like the warrior type Indians which are depicted in old western movies. Pueblo Indians were mostly farmers. Many were of the Catholic faith and were influenced by the Spanish settlers. We developed a friendship with many of the people in the art district. It was their tradition to celebrate their chosen saint every year. Also, Christmas was a big celebration, and Mike and I enjoyed celebrating with them.

To increase our packaging business I decided to network in Albuquerque, New Mexico. Even then I saw the importance of showing up and asking about other businesses. I joined and became a member of the Albuquerque Hispano Chamber of Commerce, and also became part of their ambassador group. I showed up at almost every event and asked the members what the Chamber could do to support them. I was voted by my peers to be the Vice President of the Chamber Ambassadors. My efforts paid off as I discovered our packaging business started to improve.

Considering it was just after the economic downturn of 2008, it was remarkable that we could turn the business around. The small area we were renting in the industrial area was too small for our packaging business. So Mike was able to find a larger building and move. He expanded our clientele to meet their needs in the area of industrial packaging.

During the time I was volunteering with the chamber, I learned the value of marketing and was able to apply what I learned to help our packaging business. I was grateful for what we had built in New Mexico. Although we had a nice home, and friends we enjoyed, I still missed my home in California and the opportunities that were available to me in quality assurance.

One of our clients was especially happy with Mike's talent to package the Native American artwork. They needed to ship pieces of their valuable works to Washington DC for an exhibit. Many pieces were fragile and she knew Mike would do a good job. After that, we were invited to one of her shows and I learned a great deal about Native American art.

About this time, one of our clients introduced me to a product I really liked. It was an anti-aging night cream by Nerium. At first, I was skeptical, but they told me if I didn't like it I could get my money back. I thought, *What do I have to lose?* I got amazing results. Because the sun is very harsh in New Mexico and I was concerned about the effects on my face, I was really happy with the product and how it made my skin look and feel. I actually looked a few years younger!

People noticed how nice I looked, and gave me unsolicited compliments. So I learned more about the business and ended up joining. I thought, *What do I have to lose?* If I like it, others would like it. The next time we had a family get-together, and we took a family photograph. Our friend who took the photos thought I was the youngest in our family because of my skin. When I told him, "No, I am the oldest". He didn't believe me, and said, "Your skin looks really good."

I loved Nerium's philosophies, the products, and the people were very positive. I became active with Nerium as a business, not just as a customer. People love the products for their skin. And another product I have come to appreciate helps you with brain health. I really enjoy the personal growth and development that is emphasized in most network marketing companies. Nerium was no exception. I really wanted to make an impact on people's lives. When your skin looks good, and you get compliments you feel happy, what better business could there be.

With my type of personality and scientific mind, I can appear serious. This causes some people to misunderstand me, so personal development training has really helped me be more relatable. I love learning how to be a better me. I had never been in sales or recruited people. But I thought, *What do I have to lose?* If they will show me how, and I could learn. I couldn't believe the price to get started compared to the price to start the packaging business. It seemed like a no brainer to me.

Joining Nerium was definitely pushing me out of my comfort zone, and yet I really enjoyed it. I really liked that the products were based on science. This was the first time I was doing something that I needed to develop new skills and was not using my microbiology and science education. I also had a realization that I had been growing my skills to relate to people for many years. One was networking with businesspeople while I was in New Mexico. As a Hispano Chamber volunteer in Albuquerque, I learned the skills I needed to connect with people.

While living in New Mexico, the business economy is a circular economy. Many of our clients that brought us a good income we're dependent on government and military contracts. When they lost their contracts, our business suffered. As a result, we lost the majority of our business income in early 2013 because of the loss of government contracts in the area.

In August 2013, Mike was offered an attractive position to run a packaging company in Orange County, California, and we still owned a home in the area. So we made a difficult decision, to close our packaging business in New Mexico and moved back to Orange County. This gave me an opportunity to put into practice all that I learned in New Mexico. I joined The Heart Link Network in Laguna Niguel and also other networking groups. The added bonus was making new friends.

Life Lessons: your reflection

A thought to inspire you

"Life is about creating new opportunities, not waiting for them to come to you." Selma Hayek

What does this mean in your life? ....

....

....

....

....

Reflections to Empower you:

What opportunities have presented themselves to you and have caused you

to grow in ways you hadn't expected?..

....

....

....

....

How have you prepared for times when your options seem to be fewer than

before? ....

....

....

....

....

In what ways have you needed to "pivot" your thinking to become successful? ....

....

....

....

Reflections to apply in your life: ....

....

....

....

....

....

....

....

....

....

....

*"Be persistent to achieve your goals and be flexible
about your methods of achieving them."*

Angeline Benjamin

CHAPTER 13

Learning To Adapt in California

*"All our dreams can come true
if we have the courage to pursue them."*
Walt Disney

We moved back to California with our fur-family, just before Christmas 2013. We had Lucky our Rottweiler-Lab mix, Duke our Shepherd mix, Lance our Doberman-Lab mix, and my sister's Husky-Lab mix, Lola. Because she was living in an apartment at the time and couldn't have a dog we had her join our family. I drove my Honda van and our four dogs, they were great traveling companions. Dogs don't really care if they move, as long as they are with those they love. Lance was very protective of me yet lovable, and never aggressive towards me. Duke just loved to play with both of us and liked to be a police for all the dogs. Lucky was a guard dog she would guard our home and not let anyone in unless we gave her permission. Yet when she was outside, she was friendly and let kids pet her.

It was a nice drive back to California. I was happy to be closer to my sister Bernadette and my brother Johan, as we settled into our previous home.

Moving from New Mexico on a large piece of property, back to California on a smaller residential property, proved to have some challenges. Our home insurance in California was at a premium, because of the breed of dogs we owned. It was a small price to have our family together.

A few months after settling down in California we started to have challenges with one of our next-door-neighbors. It was the four dogs we returned with, they were not happy with them. Understandably, four large breed dogs at one house is a lot for a neighborhood. When we lived next to them prior to going to New Mexico, they seemed to like our dogs, Bruno and Bronson. Maybe it was because we had two more? Maybe because they were not friendly Labs, or because they were more of a protective breed. We really didn't know for sure. Duke and Lance did not like our neighbors either, the feeling was mutual. We knew they didn't hate dogs, because their son had two labs. We knew we needed to take responsibility, but also work out an amicable compromise.

The next-door neighbor's household seemed different and was not as friendly towards us as they had been before we left. We found out that she was grieving the loss of her father, and her mother was not doing well. Possibly her tolerance to having the dogs next door was not as it once was because she was under a great deal of stress. As I have gotten older myself, my perspective on some things like this has changed, especially caring for aging parents.

Mike and I made the decision that the dogs were our family and we would not give them up or abandon them because of the neighbors. My sister's dog, Lola, was nearly fifteen and suffered arthritis in her hips. She had a good spirit in spite of her pain. She still had a good appetite and loved going on walks.

Our neighbors were resentful of our dogs and they threatened to report us to the homeowner's association. I knew we couldn't ignore the situation and it wasn't going to go away. So I thought I would approach them with negotiation in mind. I asked them, "What can we do to make this better?" Their response was for us to keep the dogs from barking. Duke and Lance especially seemed to be a threat to them. They asked us to keep them away from the wall that joined the two yards. I agreed to do my best with these two things.

One solution was to hire a professional dog trainer to help us train our dogs not to bark at certain things. The trainer wanted to know why he was being hired. We told him about the barking problem. He said with a slight smile, "Well, barking is normal for dogs." He explained that they communicate by barking.

Of course, we knew barking was their way of communication, so my thought was to compromise in some other way. Maybe, reducing their barking when the neighbors were outside. We knew the husband was a consultant and he traveled to the San Jose area each week. He was gone from Monday until Thursday evening. He didn't seem to be bothered as much. I started to pay more attention to when our neighbors were home and when they were not. I secured the dogs' door to the backyard so we could control when they were allowed outside. We made sure we took them for walks regularly. The dogs adapted to the new conditions very easily. We knew they would still need regular exercise. In New Mexico, our yard was much larger, and they could easily run in the yard. Now, the backyard was much smaller, so they needed to exercise by going on longer or more frequent walks.

Lola's health was starting to decline, it was harder for her to walk, and we were taking her to the vet more often. We even looked into places that adopted older dogs to relieve the tension between us and our neighbors. But we had no luck because of her age. Her appetite had decreased, and she seemed stressed with trying to keep up with the three younger dogs. She was also having trouble getting upstairs to sleep with all of us each night.

One day while at the vet, she explained Lola was in a lot of pain and suggested her quality of life was declining significantly. We knew what she was telling us was true, we could see she was in a lot of pain, even though we were giving her pain killers every day. We felt it was cruel to keep her living, but it was a very hard decision for us to make. It was in the best interest of Lola, we knew we needed to say good-bye to her. She had no quality of life. She barely could eat, sleep, or walk. She did not want to be around our other dogs because of her pain.

Dogs have such a simple life. They don't ask for too much, food, companionship, and exercise. Our trainer told us not to feel bad for them, they don't really need a lot, and they adapt very well to a changing environment. A short walk, and a treat when we return, makes them so happy!

The trainer suggested a bark collar. It is a device that gives the dog slight electrical jolt air times when their bark is not wanted. It does not hurt them, but it sends them a message. They learned very quickly that in certain situations we didn't want them to bark.

The neighbors saw we were trying very hard to accommodate their wishes, and although we were never friends or socialized with them they left us alone. The other neighbors were always friendly, their dog had passed away before we returned from New Mexico, so they seemed to enjoy seeing our dogs. They never complained about our dogs at all.

Life is like hills and valleys, we all experience both ups and downs. We learn in the valleys, and we earn the hills, that's life. In networking, I participate in the things that lift you up. I don't listen to negative journalism because it can cause you to become negative, even fearful. Staying away from negative influences was a suggestion of a mentor, and it works for me.

Having a dog is a positive influence in my life, they are such a pleasure. They are grateful for the simple things. Dogs are always happy to see you, they don't hold grudges and they easily learn to adapt to new situations. They enjoy their life and it is a pleasure to have them be a part of mine. I have worked to educate and inspire people about having dogs and adopting dogs. When I see elderly people who are so lonely, I suggest a small dog.

According to agingcare.com, having a pet can reduce the feeling of loneliness, reduce blood pressure, give a person a purpose and the dogs repay their owners with unconditional love.

One more added benefit of dog ownership is they encourage their owners to exercise. By reminding their owner that it is time to go for a walk. It is a mutual benefit to both the dog and the owner. I know from experience that having a dog to pet, take them for a walk, feed them, and just hug them to reduce your stress and keep you from being lonely. That is why Mike and I go on doggy vacation once a year even if it is a short weekend getaway. If a person suffers from allergies, there are breeds that are hypoallergenic.

If you don't like dogs, you might consider getting a cat. One thing that is different, they don't go for walks, so they might be better if the person is more sedentary. And there are even a few breeds that are also hypoallergenic.

If you are a dog lover, I would recommend you watch two of my favorite movies: Hachi: A dog's tale (based on a story of "Hachiko" the true story of a loyal dog) and A Dog's purpose. Both are available in book form as well. These works will help you understand why dogs have a special place in my heart.

Back to Orange County

Meanwhile, I wanted to expand my Nerium business, so I knew I needed to network. I had learned about this in New Mexico. Show up, ask, and help others. Do it over and over again. The most important question to ask, "What can I do to help you?" Networking companies like Nerium, invest so much in developing the people who join. Personal development is very important when it comes to business success and also networking. Many network marketing companies spend a lot of time and money on growing people and learning the importance of a positive mindset. This is how I was able to learn from John Maxwell, Darren Hardy, and others as they were keynote speakers at the Nerium's conferences. For the first time, I bought their books to continue learning.

I joined Heart Link Network in Orange County. This is an international organization, which is dedicated to showcasing, advertising, enriching, and empowering professional women in business in order for them to create heartfelt, meaning relationships with one another. I have grown to love this group very much. I've really enjoyed the women who were involved in this group because they are easy to talk to and many have positive attitudes. Caprice Crebar is the chapter leader in Laguna Niguel, California, and she is amazing, she embodies all of the ideals of Heart Link and embraces the members and guests.

Another group I joined was the Orange County Networker. I was a solution-oriented member, I helped increase the number of people who attended the meeting while I was the Program Chairperson. I worked on the meetings being more organized and changing some of the structure of the meeting and programs. I then served the group as the vice president.

After being in the group for about a year, they had seen my leadership qualities, so they asked me to run for the president of the group. According to their By-laws, I could only be a president for one term.

I also joined the local chamber in Mission Viejo Chamber of Commerce and joined their ambassador group. Also, I was active in the other chamber of commerce groups in my area, like Rancho Santa Margarita. I did some volunteer work and helped the president with some of the ideas that had worked in other groups.

Through my years with Neora (formerly Nerium) organization I have learned to embrace the importance of personal development. Our mindset is most important when it comes to success. What you do, what you like and dislike is because of our mindset. By nature, I am an optimistic person. I have learned to stay away from negative people because after some time it becomes irritating, and so when I want to stay focused on my goals, and investing in people, I look for people like me, that have a positive outlook. Nerium then changed their name to Neora as they expanded their product lines.

Networking, I have found, is an important part of my business, I meeting people and help them with their goals and objectives. Learning ways to meet people and connect with people is so important to building a business.

As I have learned how to network, I have also realized I love coaching people. I look for motivated people who have goals and want to get things done. In a company such as Neora, it is possible to grow a large team of people who also want to invest in others and build a great team of people. By building a team, all of you are working towards fulfilling your dreams. I found that I enjoy coaching more than sales. Selling is merely sharing what we do, and through this I end up coaching people and recruiting them into the business, that is working in my strength zone.

When I coach a person, I have found some of them have way too many excuses. I will not allow my clients or my team members to give me excuses, not if they have told me they are committed to the success of their business. I can also say, my coaching style is not for everyone, but it is for everyone who wants to succeed and who is open to dispelling excuses. I am a matter of fact coach, I will call you on your excuses to help you see them, so you will not use them to get in the way of your success.

When I took my StrengthFinder assessment, it confirmed to me that my top five strengths are: Achiever, Focus, Learner, Analytical, and Responsibility.

I would like to encourage you to take the time you need to find a career or business that will push you to fulfill your passion. By using online assessments you may discover where your personality might fit in the job world.

Life Lessons: your reflection

A thought to inspire you:

"Your background and circumstances may have influenced who you are but you are responsible for who you become." Darren Hardy

What does this mean in your life? ....

....

....

....

Reflections to empower you:

Have you needed to negotiate with someone to make it a win-win

situation? ....

....

....

....

Have you needed to take responsibility for a choice you made that others didn't agree with? ....

....

....

....

Has your dog (or pet) changed your outlook on life? ....

....

....

Reflections: what will you apply in your life? ....

....

....

....

....

....

....

....

....

....

....

....

....

....

....

....

"Look for a way to achieve your goals rather than looking for excuses.

Angeline Benjamin

CHAPTER 14

A New Home Town

"If you don't go after what you want, you'll never have it.
If you don't ask, the answer is always no.
If you don't step forward, you're always in the same place."
Nora Roberts

Then, Mike got a new job working for a luxury car maker. The company was owned by a billionaire who had a dream to build a car company in the United States. It was his belief that there was a market for his design which costs the consumer over $100,000, not a car for everyone. He purchased a bankrupt car company in Orange County, and they needed a packaging engineer, and Mike was perfect for the job with his experience with aeronautics and industrial packaging. His expertise is very rare. I told Mike, "Sometimes things happen for a reason." The cars are handmade, not built fully computerized as is done in larger manufacturers such as General Motors. They only made a few cars a week. His job was in their warehouse which was located in Moreno Valley.

It was a difficult commute for Mike, nearly two hours one way to our home and to his job. Before deciding to move, we wanted to make sure he liked his new employer and his new job. The commute was hard on him. He would leave our home at five in the morning and not return until five in the evening. Over time he became more and more fatigued. He was taking his motorcycle for an easier commute on the highway, but this was also more dangerous.

We made the decision to move closer to Mike's employment. Although I loved Orange County, I also knew I could work anywhere. My office was at home, I could drive to Orange County when needed, and also network in my new area. We started looking for areas that would work the best for us to live south of Moreno Valley. One area we were looking at was Murietta, my niece lived in the area. A nearby area that was recommended to us was Menifee, and it was a shorter commute for Mike. The homes were perfect for our needs and it was close to Murrieta, where were already have some familiarity and family, so it was a good place for us to move.

We decided to sell our home in Orange County. I used a realtor that I met through networking. It was a challenge when we had our first open house because I needed to have the dogs with me for the whole day. After the open house, we received a cash offer right away. As I had previously learned, everything is negotiable. I insisted they pay a little bit more than proposed, the house was in good shape, and plus we wanted 30-day escrow. That gave us only one week to pack and vacate our house after the closing of escrow. This was a great advantage for them, however, we also knew, a cash offer was less likely to fall out of escrow. We made the deal, but then we needed a place to move.

After our "neighbor experience" in Orange County, we wanted to make sure we moved to a dog-friendly neighborhood. We found the perfect home for us and the timing was ideal. The home we chose was a great size for us. It had a large back yard, walking trails, and parks for our walks with the dogs. As you may know, the timing of two homes in escrow at the same time can be challenging. But, the timing ended up working for us especially considering the move of our family with three dogs. Although we moved from what the realtors told us was a desirable neighborhood, for us, our new home was better all the way around.

In our new home, I took time out to get settled in. This time my goals were not work-related, however, the same principles applied. We needed things for the interior and the exterior of our new home. Much of what I worked on was something I didn't need Mike's input on, however, I checked with him regularly to make sure he was good with the decisions I was making. He was working full time and I didn't want to overwhelm him with the small details that were easy to manage. He trusted my judgment, so the only things that I thought mattered to him, I made sure he was in the loop.

My goal was, by the end of 2017, I wanted to have a plan for the backyard, window coverings, and new bedroom furniture. My goals were written, with a completion date. Neither of us wanted boxes sitting around, so I needed to unpack. Even when you don't have the plan fully developed, it is okay to have a date to work on parts of your plan.

All of the areas we needed to complete we worked on regularly. We found window coverings and had them installed. We found bedroom furniture and had it delivered. We found contractors to do the back yard. Our front yard landscaping had been done by the builder before we moved in, however, Mike wanted to make some improvements. We scheduled the work to improve our front yard to be completed in early 2018, it was assigned to Mike because he knew what he wanted and could work on it after work and on the weekends. Our dogs loved our new home, they saw other dogs walking in front of our home, and especially Lucky and Duke were excited to interact. Lance, as usual, he liked to stay near me. We love going for a walk with our dogs around our neighborhood.

Now that we were in our new community and I had gotten settled into our new home. I thought it was time to get back into my business networking in the new area. When I was living in Orange County I had met Joan Wakeland, I remembered that she had mentioned she lived in the area where I had now moved. She had told me about the National Association of Female Executives (NAFE) group that met in Menifee. So I decided to go to the meeting and look for Joan to meet up with her again. The meeting was led by Robbie Motter, I had looked at three other NAFE meetings and she was leading them as well. I thought she has a lot of energy to run three meetings. The meeting was close to my home. After going to the meeting, I met another lady who I also knew from networking in Orange County. Robbie was welcoming and cordial. They spoke to me about joining the group and told me about the advantages of membership. One thing that had appealed to me was I could go to the other chapter meetings and pay as a member. The price of the membership was reasonable. My mind started calculating and I realized by becoming a member was to my advantage. I thought, *Why not? What do I have to lose?* It was a no brainer.

Robbie was very genuine, and she loved connecting me to people. She was very impressive at 82, and I wanted to get to know her better. I thought, *I must attend more of her meetings.* I saw Robbie again at the next meeting and she introduced me to many more people. Each time Robbie was always willing to help me and the others. She loves to connect people to those who can help you. I saw that she had some skills that I wanted to cultivate. So I observed how she interacted with me and the other ladies. The longer I spent time with Robbie the more I saw her genuine approach and energetic nature.

The following month, I went back to the Menifee Nafe meeting, and this time I saw Joan Wakeland whom I had looked for at the previous month's meeting. One thing I heard Robbie say was, "Just Show Up!" I thought she was right, I liked showing up to meet new people, and where ever Robbie went she would invite me and I really loved getting to know the ladies in her network.

After getting to know Robbie more, I found out that she was the founder of another organization, the Global Society for Female Entrepreneurs (GSFE), a non-profit organization that helps women in business. She let me know when she was doing fundraising and when I could, I would show up to help. Come to find out that was her signature statement, "Just show up, you never know what treasure you will find."

At each meeting, she would talk about events she has attended and the great things that came out of them. I decided I like showing up! It seemed like everyone in my new area knew Robbie. I went to all of the events and meetings that she was at. I started volunteering my time to help her. I would show up early and ask what can I do to help. She would assign me to check-in people, or welcome people. I liked doing this for her.

One area I wanted to grow in is connecting with women, this is an area I am working on personally. I want to be a better listener. I can be overpowering and I can intimidate people. I don't want to do that. Hanging out with Robbie, I found is a great way to expand my business. Sometimes Robbie would have an extra ticket to an event and she would give it to me. She would say, "Be my guest." I went to events I had never attended before.

Robbie taught me to "Show up and ask." That's her motto! I am not as good at the asking part as I am with the showing up part. We sometimes have a difficult time asking, and we don't want to be a burden to someone. Robbie tells me, "How will you know if they can help you if you don't ask?" She explained it is important to let people know what you want. Otherwise, they won't know. This makes perfect sense to me. I believe when you ask for something like a referral you need to followup. Eventually, your reputation would follow you if you don't, and people will stop giving you things. When someone gives me something I know it is important to follow up. That is the commitment you make when you accept what they have given to you. If I tell someone I will be there, I go. I have made a commitment. I learn to be organized with my commitments, and the only time I wouldn't live up to my word would be an emergency, an accident, or something that happens unexpectedly that I need to take care of and I will follow-up with them when I get a chance - so they know they can trust me.

Commitment is a big deal, my parents taught me this as a child. I know in Southern California people hesitate to commit. Robbie explained this to me, she said, "If someone commits and doesn't show up, they feel bad. So it is easier not to commit in the first place. If they decide not to go, or if something better comes up they don't feel bad not showing up." This gave me another way to look at it. In California, it seems people rarely RSVP for networking events. However in the corporate world if people showed up without an RSVP they may not be able to get into the event. Some people just show up, and of course, the host is happy to see them. Some may think this is being open-minded. I think it is inconsiderate. She explained to me not to judge, just be happy they are there. I think in some cultures, people don't think to RSVP. If there is a cost involved, people RSVP. But for free events, people don't. This doesn't make sense to me because I want to make sure I register so I can get into the event. When I RSVP, it is my word that I will attend, and this is my reputation even if it is free. People learn they can rely on you, your word is important in business.

I also learned from another mentor don't expect people to buy what you are selling at a networking event. You are there to build relationships not to sell. You must show up seven to ten times before people think to buy something from you. If you get lucky and people buy on the first time you attend an event, this is not a normal occurrence. People don't buy a service or a product because you are unique, they buy your service or product because they know, like, and trust you! Or they may have been referred to you by someone they know, like, and trust, and this helps them make the decision.

Many people sell the same products, each time I go to a networking event I meet people in the same or similar businesses. I believe in what I do, I know I provide exceptional service, I have been in the business for a long time I have confidence in my ability and in my products. My reputation is one that I take care of my customers. This also helps a customer decide to do business with me. Unless the product is very rare, they might not have a choice. I don't know of any businesses like that.

I try to be honest with myself, and I want to do the things I am good at, and I don't get frustrated when I am telling someone about the business if they aren't interested. The timing makes a big difference. When I first heard about Nerium skincare I was skeptical, I didn't see the vision for the long term business beyond the product. Was it going to work for me? I didn't know. I understand other people might feel the same way. It wasn't until later that I saw the business as something I could be passionate about. I believed in the product, I saw how it was helping me. I came into the business gradually. Then when you can see how you can help people get out of debt, or go on a much-needed vacation, anything they would want to do with some extra money earned from their efforts. It is powerful. In uncertain times it pays to have a Plan B. When you see that, you are unstoppable! Your passion for what you do becomes evident and you attract the people you want to work with, naturally.

I have so much passion for coaching people who want to be helped and they know what they want. I will go the extra mile to help them. There is no greater satisfaction than to help people achieve something they might not have accomplished without a coach.

I have learned I need more patience with those who haven't decided what they want, and they are asking for help. I have learned if you don't want something bad enough to work for it, I can't help you. No one can, and you are just fooling yourself. I don't have the passion to recruit people for the business unless they want it bad enough to get through the challenges, the tough times, And will grow themselves.

Robbie has been a great mentor to help me reframe looking at those who are not as evolved. I know I shouldn't judge people, we are all at different stages of life. But I do have difficulties with people who have no goals. I must be honest with myself, and know what clients I enjoy working with. I also need to be honest and go the networking events where I enjoy the people who attend.

Joan Wakeland has become a friend and mentor. Her skills as a mentor are completely different from Robbie. She is less direct and has more patience around indecisive people or women who need a lot of personal attention. She is able to talk to anyone and enjoys getting to know people. I need both of them, each one provides me with certain qualities I need. I follow Robbie because I respect her. I can be very stubborn at times, and this is a part of my personality. I also need to understand there are times when I need to say no when I am asked to help. But also, I am willing to do more for those I respect.

In another area of my life that I have a coach is at the gym. She is easy to talk to and motivating. She coaches me on the simple ways to work out. Also, I have found, I enjoy yoga, and the instructor is another coach for me. A good coach and a good instructor will motivate you. This is a skill that I need with exercise, and through them, I realize I need to motivate my clients as they have done for me.

Through my coaches and mentors, I have learned motivation is a big part of coaching the clients I have. I must empower my clients to be their best self, and then motivate them to stay the course. After all, FOCUS can be an acrostic for Follow One Course Until Successful!

My Neora business is a perfect example. Deep down in my heart, I don't have the passion to recruit people. I didn't really know that until I was already in the business. I had tried another network marketing business but I hadn't needed to recruit people. I didn't understand the process. One of the reasons I wanted to be a part of the business was to learn and be mentored by the leader, Jeff Olson.

Network marketing has a focus on personal development which is a benefit of belonging to this type of business and is also very rewarding. No matter what business you are in, of course, you will want to make money, but your growth is also important and rewarding. Without passion for what you do, it will be hard to accomplish your goals.

Each person has a definition of success, and it isn't necessarily a certain amount of money. Whatever you think it is, it is for you. If another person's definition isn't like yours, it isn't right or wrong. It is a personal philosophy. For me, I needed to be honest with myself, and I needed to decide what would it mean to me to be a success.

My ideas may be very different from some other person's ideas. I may not have the same goals as my friends in network marketing. Regardless if your goals are to make money or not, do you want to share the product? Do you want to recruit? Otherwise, why would you be in business? Those are not the bottom line results I am seeking. I have had people who I have turned down to be a part of my team. I knew my team wasn't the right team for them. I didn't respect them, and I knew I couldn't help them. One of the main reasons for this is I didn't see the motivation I know they will need to be successful. I don't want to waste my time investing in them. I am a work in progress when it comes to being patient and having more empathy.

There are people who begin their complaints before we even get started, I don't have the patience to listen to them. When their negative comments about spending time in the business doing the things that will help them succeed, and are only concerned about the money, they can be on someone's else team that has the patience to work with them.

I have learned I am unique in this approach. I know I have gotten results with the products I have used. I love how my skin looks, and I feel good, I know this is due to the products I use. It isn't the system of success I have been taught, which is to sell products and recruit. So I realized, maybe I don't have the passion to do the business through recruiting. I was taught this was the way to make money on this business.

I was more interested in coaching. If they need a guide in the business, and they want to make a difference in the lives of others, and in their own life. I might be able to help them. They will need to know, I am a no excuses and no-nonsense coach. I know myself, I just don't have the patience for people who are lazy, and don't want to work, or have no goals.   That is my philosophy, and I learned from my mentor you earn what you want, it is the fruits of your labor in life.

When someone asks me if my products work, I don't immediately say "yes". I say, "It depends."   It depends on you, your skin, your body because everyone is different. It might not work for everyone. I wasn't taught to say it this way.   I just wanted to share the product, and I will tell people how it works for me. I let people know the benefits if they don't get excited that is okay with me.

When I tried it for the first time, I wanted to get a result. So I tried it, and I did get results. I will tell people, it normally works. But for some, it may not work, and if it doesn't work for you in 30 days, you can get your money back. People started noticing after I used it for 30 days, that sold me. When I was given this information I thought, *What do I have to lose?* The worst thing that could happen, I would get my money back. I have tried many things that didn't work. I have no problem telling someone "no," if I don't want their products. AND I'll say "Yes," if their products or services work for me.

I have learned most people won't ask for their money back, they are not comfortable asking as I am. If someone tells me I can have my money back, that is their promise to me. My personality, my life lessons, being mentored, and being confident this doesn't bother me.

Growing up my parents told us, "Life isn't always fair, you have to work for what you want." If you don't know what you want, find someone to guide you. The only way this works, you must have the desire first. Without desire, you won't be successful. The first thing we do is protect ourselves by saying, "No." Our minds can talk us out of things, that is why we need a mentor and a coach

People are inherently good, I believe that many people will want to help you. But it needs to be the right person. Not everyone is able to help you in the right way. If you ask someone and they don't want to help you, find someone who genuinely does.

My parents also taught me you can't hold people's hands the whole time helping them get someplace. If someone wants to accomplish something give them enough to get up on their own feet, then encourage them to continue. The bottom line is, it is their journey and they will enjoy the fruits of their accomplishments if they work for them. They need initiative and drive to get what they want. You can't give it to them, don't make them helpless. Inspire, empower, and educate them, let them walk on their own two feet, they will appreciate it more. I learned from my mentor, we give them encouragement and help them see their value and help them to have self-worth.

My appreciation for what I have comes from my early childhood. My parents could afford to buy us many toys, but they knew if they did we wouldn't learn to appreciate what we had. If we only had one doll, we learned to appreciate it. If we wanted more we could earn it. They taught us the importance of being educated so we could work for what we had, by earning it, and the value of education which gave us the ability to earn our way in life. As I have gone through life, all of my mentors were of the same philosophy so I am fortunate and blessed that I have learned that appreciation at a young age.

I know what I want, I don't want anyone to hold my hand, or to do it for me. I want to do it, and experience the satisfaction of knowing I did my job well. I know I will enjoy the accomplishment even more. I am nearly 69 years old, at the time of writing this book, and I am still learning. I feel like I will always want to learn more, keep moving forward. I want to inspire everyone to enjoy the fruits of life as I have done and I hope to empower you and educate you to take that next step to move forward even if you aren't sure how to get there. You will find people to help you, just show up, ask, and take action towards what you want, it is simple and yet it has worked well for me.

We are responsible for ourselves and the actions we take. If it doesn't work, well, try it again. Don't blame others for the things you are responsible for, own your mistakes. By doing that you will move forward and not get stuck in the past. Mistakes don't cost you anything except to teach you more. But if you keep making the same mistakes over and over again, then you know you are not learning from them.

As I go through my life experience, I know having effective coaches help us accomplish our goals. If you consider Olympic athletes, they all have effective coaches. Every program I have seen, and books I have read about successful people, they mention their mentors and coaches. To accomplish their goals, they have discipline and they have a plan and their coaches have kept them in the game.

I thank all of my mentors and coaches that have helped me accomplish my goals, without them I couldn't have achieved the success in life I am proud of today.

Life Lessons: your reflection

A thought to inspire you:

"To be yourself in a world that is constantly trying to make you something else is the greatest accomplishment." Ralph Waldo Emerson

What does this mean in your life? ....

....

....

....

Reflections to empower you:

What challenges have you needed to accept that have come into your life?

....

....

....

....

What ways have you needed to look for the positive in negative

circumstances? ....

....

....

How can you get out of your comfort zone and experience new opportunities

for growth? ....

....

....

Reflections: what will you apply in your life? ....

....

....

....

....

....

....

....

....

....

....

....

....

....

....

"Know what you want, and then ask for it."

Angeline Benjamin

CHAPTER 15

Value Having Mentors and Coaches

*"The delicate balance of mentoring someone is
not creating them in your own image,
but giving them the opportunity to create themselves."*
Steven Spielberg

My first thoughts about having mentors began with my father's stories of his early experiences. He never explained them in a way that we understood by the definition of a mentor. He described them as more as his experiences and how people helped him so he could achieve his goals. They were willing to inspire him, educate him, and empowered him. Today I see these people in my life as mentors and coaches.

My father mentioned to me that his first employer taught him valuable lessons when he was young. His first mentor, he would call a teacher, inspired him to have stock in the company and save his earnings so eventually he would have the money to start his own company.

His teachers in school educated him, and the officer in the Japanese Army taught him the language, more teaching than mentoring, yet he also mentored him. He didn't have a lot of good words to say about the Japanese occupation of Indonesia, however, he did talk about the benefits that he gained under the mentorship of the officer. He trusted my father to learn Japanese so he would be of value as an interpreter.

My father's gregarious personality, his drive, and his natural talents helped him achieve these goals. He made many sacrifices to achieve what he wanted, he was very tenacious, his modeling influenced me. As he told his life stories I learned about his mentors. He didn't actually tell me he had mentors, I learned how he valued the people who invested in him. He also taught me that mistakes are okay, as long as you learn from them.

One of the biggest lessons I learned from my father's life was don't believe what people predict about your future. This was in the case of the fortune-teller that told his mother that he wouldn't be a successful son. He never accepted this about himself. You are in charge of your future no matter who has said what about you. My mom also told me that just because someone is smart, or intelligent, or has a high IQ, this doesn't mean they will be successful. How you are raised, and how you use your intelligence and learn to work for what you want plays a big role in your success.

Some parents treat their children differently when they are very smart and have a high IQ. This was the case with my father's mother. When a person is spoiled by their parents, rather than showing them the value of working for what they want, this is a disservice to the child. They don't learn the value of working. This was the case of my father's two older brothers. They never learned the basics to be successful in life because they were pampered. In adulthood, they had no ambition.

My parents were my first mentors, like most kids. They didn't have a college education because of the war. But they had common sense, and what we now might refer to as EQ or emotional intelligence. This gave them what they needed to succeed. My father had wanted to go to college, this is why they worked so hard to ensure that my siblings and I could get the education they were not able to have. Papi always made sure we had the books we needed or anything that was education-related. He felt toys were not valuable, they did not help you better yourself, they were only for play. For example, they didn't understand why I wanted more dolls, they felt one was enough. This is how I grew up and I am grateful for their values. They taught me the value of money and prioritizing it towards education. The rest was up to us.

Growing up, nothing came easy for me. I was an above-average student, not exceptional or genius because I studied hard I got good grades. My parents helped me with guidelines and direction, and yes, it was because I was in the right environment. This helped me become who I am. In the old Chinese culture, many parents feel that if you are not a doctor or engineer, you won't have success in your life, I have seen that this isn't true. Even if you are not smart in math and science doesn't mean you will not be a success. Success comes from how diligent you are, and how hard you push your self to succeed.

If your teacher is someone who teaches, guides and lifts you up by virtue of his or her experience and insight. They're usually someone a little farther ahead of you on the path—though that doesn't always mean they're older! They can be a mentor that truly impacts your life. With their insights and experience, they guide you by building trust and modeling behaviors. An effective mentor understands that his or her role is to be dependable, engaged, authentic, and tuned into the needs of their mentee.

When I was younger, and early in my career, I didn't understand the role and the benefits of being mentored until I had someone who was willing to invest their time and knowledge in me. I had teachers, but their role is blurred when it comes to mentoring and coaching. They teach a curriculum and the expectation is you learn the curriculum, and then you are tested to ensure you have retained what you have learned.

When I look back in my life, having a mentor who inspired me, and empowered me, and made sure I received an education, this is what contributed to my successful life. As I have looked back on my education and my job experiences, having a mentor was something I didn't see the value it gave me until after I succeed and reflected on my success.

Now, let's talk about how a coach can help you. The right **coach** helps you accelerate your learning, improve critical thinking skills, improve your leadership skills, interactions within and outside of a team. They help you with your blind spots and increase self-awareness.

A coach equips you to lead from wherever you are and helps you gain personal clarity as you answer thought-provoking questions about your values, purpose, and goals, you will develop practical habits as you learn to apply new insights. Your coach holds you accountable as you reinforce positive change through action. The right coach will empower you to be responsible for your life's decisions and see a path to take control of your life and learn to be consistent and intentional about your personal growth.

My teachers in high school, professors in college, graduate school professor, first supervisor and managers at Hunt-Wesson, and the Quality Assurance Directors at Denny's, Yum Brands, and Taco Bell, all have coached me. They also taught me valuable life lessons, not just in my career or education, but in my personal life. In fact, when I was at Taco Bell, the company invested in me and trained me to be an effective coach when I taught food safety workshops and also when I visited restaurants. They taught me to be more of a coach rather than an enforcer or an auditor. Some of my former bosses helped me be a better employee, and also a better person.

Some of the people I worked with throughout my career focused on development within my job performance, enhancing what I already had learned. What made some of the leaders in the corporate setting better, was how they cared and invested their time in my development, not just a boss who was in charge. The majority of the people that were my bosses invested in me as my coach, helping me see the value I brought with confidence and trust in me. In turn, I was able to invest in those I was leading, making an impact on their lives.

At times I've heard some people say they hate their bosses, but for me I felt I wanted to focus on the positive. Of course, there were a few I did not respect, even a few I didn't like, but I always looked at the good they could teach me.

One mentor I want to mention is Julia Stewart. After college, she spent 18 years in various Marketing positions with increasing levels of responsibility. She wanted to be a CEO but instinctively knew no one would afford her the opportunity to run a company unless she had Operations experience. So she started at the bottom at Taco Bell in their Advanced Management Recruit (AMR) program as an assistant manager of a restaurant! Six years later, she was running the entire franchise organization! I learned more about her and she gained my respect over time.

She taught me that education was a foundation of your career, but the experience was learning the work itself. We really liked each other, I asked her to mentor me unofficially. I didn't want people to think I was showing off somehow, but I valued her as a friend and a successful executive. She has great self-worth, confidence, and made difficult decisions. She was willing to take the risk and was able to communicate effectively to get the results she wanted. This what inspired me to learn more from her.

She was a very driven businesswoman, her focus was on marketing and operations. She also knew food quality and safety was important to the operation. She helped me see the value of what I brought to the organization. She saw my passion. She invited me many times to tour restaurants with her. She valued my knowledge, opinion, and education, and I valued hers. I saw her attention to detail, and how she would work in the restaurants, some would not listen, and were negative, or thought they knew better than the experts. She would take a calculated risk when it is necessary. She was respected, and I appreciated her mentorship. She taught me to look at someone, not because of their popularity, but of what their actions showed.

She would talk to me about skeptics, and she would encourage me to surround myself with positive people, but also the ones who were knowledgeable. She impressed upon me that no matter what your gender, you can be anything if you work for it.

She encouraged me to find a mentor and a coach to encourage me in a positive way. She shared with me her goal, which was to become a Chief Executive Officer of a major restaurant chain. She knew she was not able to get this position at Taco Bell, so she moved to Kansas to become the president of Applebee's and promised the CEO position, once she turned the company around. Once done, the Chairman took back the promise. So she left Applebee's and joined IHOP Corporation as CEO. Six years later, IHOP bought Applebees.

She formed and became the Chief Executive of DineEquity holding this position for about sixteen years. DineEquity is one of the largest casual dining companies in the world, with subsidiaries that include Applebee's and IHOP. After left DineEquity a few years ago, in early 2020, she started a wellness company, "Alurx" enabled by a technology platform providing a customized journey for wellness. In October, she launched, www.alurx.com.

After 45 years helping entrepreneurs, she became one! Julia inspired me to believe in myself, continue to work at what I wanted to achieve. Some people thought her goals were far-reaching! But she told me, "If you focus and work at it, you can achieve what you believe in." I am grateful for all of the mentors and coaches who have inspired, educated, and empowered me during my career with Taco Bell and Yum Brands, and even earlier in my career. When I decided to retire from Taco Bell Corporation and become an entrepreneur, I took their wisdom and investment with me.

Finding New Mentors and Coaches

When I was with Taco Bell I had mentors and coaches that helped me go the extra mile, further than I would have gone without them. So when I became an entrepreneur, I knew I needed to seek out mentors and coaches.

One area I found very valuable was taking assessments to learn what I didn't know about myself. Assessments are important because they assist in helping you understand, and fully know yourself, so you can have direction in developing a personal growth plan. When I was at Taco Bell I found a valuable tool, StrengthsFinder. Mr. Don Clifton, who is the founder and chief designer of the profile assessment. The department head made this a requirement for the managers.

This assessment benefitted the employees in knowing their strengths, but also the supervisors and managers benefited from knowing the strengths of their teams. It is very important to be in a position that you fully understand yourself and the strengths you bring to the table. When we all work in our strength zones we are better all around. Knowing others' strengths can help you and your organization build stronger task forces. A link to the free version is located in the references in the back of this book, I highly recommend getting the full version to use as a method of self-awareness and growth. This assessment helps you build upon your natural talents to empower yourself. It will aid in changing the areas that can help you develop your greatest talents into strengths. This helps you to build confidence. I learned through personal growth that it is important to find what you are good at and develop those areas so you can become great. If you focus on areas you are not gifted in, at best you will become average, and no one becomes really successful when they are only mediocre.

The StrengthsFinder assessment helped me find my own strengths and was full of insights that helped me with self-awareness and what was naturally and easier for me to do. I learned from my manager that it helped her also, so she could focus her coaching by knowing my top strengths and matching them with the projects she assigned to me.

I remembered how impactful the StrengthsFinder assessment was for me. So when I moved back to California and I was networking more, and I wanted to find an assessment that could help me connect with people so I could build relationships. I found "Color Code," an assessment that identifies your natural personality attributes.

The assessment was recommended to me by a Color Code coach who helped me personally, professionally, and because of this, I had my husband take it also. This helped my relationship with him because now I know him better. The color code founder Dr. Taylor Hartman, explains that people have basic traits that you can identify easier by remembering your childhood experiences which can be placed in four areas of similar traits. His expertise helped him place each of these groups of traits in four colors based on their driving core personality. For more information see a white paper, a link is provided in the references at the back of the book as well as a link to take the assessment/test.

I discovered everyone has a core personality and some have a secondary personality. It also explains the motivating force which helps you discover why you do what you do, and how it motivates you.

When I got my full assessment, which I thought was worth the small investment, I discovered my core personality is "Red." My core need is power and it motivates me from my core at 47.03%, the "Red," needs to look good technically, be right, and be respected and want to lead others and experience challenging adventure. My secondary color is "blue." The traits of "blue" are which is 30.94% of my personality. As I looked to apply the information I gained through the assessment, I realize I am sometimes passionate about things, and I am very driven, direct, and adamant especially if I think I am right. I am a strong leader, I like getting results, and I like to stay focused. The needs of the personality with primarily "blue" traits, is to have integrity and be appreciated. They are focused on quality and creating strong relationships. What this report shows is that I am motivated by a need for power, I am confident, productive, action-oriented, determined, naturally a leader, responsible, and I am very focused. However, I was told by the Color Code coach, because I have over 30% of " Blue" as my secondary category, this is the opposite of the "Red" traits. People who are primarily "Blue" are quality-oriented, detail-conscious, well mannered, nurturing, and loyal. So I can be demanding in the "Red" part of my personality and yet emotional in the "Blue." This explains my staff's confusion because one day I might have been nurturing and the next more demanding, depending on which part of my personality I was operating in.

Through assessments, I understand myself better now. Although I like to be right and have power I also value loyalty and integrity. That is why, when I was in a network marketing business. My up-line asked me, "Are you willing to do anything to achieve your goal." I had to pause a while, and I told him, "No, I am willing to work my best to achieve my goal, as long as what I do is ethical." He did not understand my answer, because to him, of course, to be successful he believes we have to be ethical. But my interpretation of "anything" meant anything! I look at the literal meaning, it means no exception. I wasn't willing to do anything but I was willing to do anything that can be included in ethical business practices.

Sometimes we like to compare information, and I decided that it had been a long time since I took the assessment offered by StrengthsFinder. So took it again. After taking it again, I had the same results. It revealed my top five areas of strength are: Achiever, Focused, Learner, Analytical, and Responsible. I thought again, this confirmed the areas of my strengths and these areas should be the ones I work on. I use this information to know myself, know areas of growth, make sure I am using my strengths, and it doesn't puzzle me anymore as to why I do what I do.

Remembering back, it all became clear to me when I took the StrengthsFinder assessment. I saw for the first time in writing my own strengths. I was proud that I was made up of strengths that have gotten me where I am today. I was able to own my strengths and be proud of who I am. Also, it is important to learn about your blind spots, some examples of mines are, being too demanding, and appearing emotionally distant. I have learned to stop and respond to interruptions from the important people in my life. I also understand and accept we all have differences and have learned how to grow, but at the same time accept my own identity.

We are all different because if we were the same, the world would be in chaos! We need everyone to be themselves. With my scientific mind, I like to get facts to share, not go with the information that might not be true, or skewed towards a particular point of view.

The Enneagram assessment has gained traction recently, however, it isn't new. Enneagram is a model of nine interconnected personality types, which has been around for 2,500 years. I recently took this assessment and it confirmed, my highest score was a tie between Type 1 (The Reformer) and Type 8 (the Challenger). My second highest score was type 3 (The Achiever). You might want to see yours, you can go to this website for your free assessment. Of course, like many of these assessments to gain a deeper understanding, there is a paid version also. I took the paid one because it was worth the small investment.

If you are interested in self-awareness and unlocking your true potential, there is another personality assessment Wired2Perform, I suggest taking it also. It is a proactive people performance management platform that combines the power of behavioral science and people analytic to help us grow, optimize, and access a more productive workforce. I took it and it shows I am an "Influencer" a similar theme with other assessments I took.

Personality assessments are very valuable in helping us understand ourselves. I recommend taking several of them to help you get to know yourself better. They can give you valuable insights about what you are good at, where your strengths are, and knowing how you are naturally equipped. Then you can use them for direction in your life, and when you do they also help you with confidence, and most importantly develop a growth plan based on the information.

As an entrepreneur, I used many methods to grow personally. It required new skills, knowledge, and wisdom. Some of which I brought with me from my previous career experience. However, I needed to grow in new areas so I looked for people who could help me. I found virtual mentors watching webinars and videos. I also read a book written by my new mentors and applied the principles I needed in my new role. When I started networking, I applied what I was learning.

Life Lessons: your reflection

A thought to inspire you:

"To have more than you've got, become more than you are." Jim Rohn

What does this mean in your life? ....

....

....

....

Reflections to Empower you:

Have you been mentored by somebody you did not realize at the time, but

later realized how they made a great impact on your life? ....

....

....

....

Have you met somebody who valued your dream or vision and encouraged
you? How did that help you? ....

....

....

....

What personality assessments have you taken, what insights about yourself

did you learn? ....

....

....

Have you discovered your blindspots and developed ways to overcome them? ....

....

....

Reflections: what will you apply in your life? ....

....

....

....

....

....

....

....

....

....

....

....

"A 'coach' and a 'mentor' is someone who carries a valued person
from where they are to where they want to be."

Angeline Benjamin

CHAPTER 16

Rewards and Challenges

"The purpose of life is to live it, to taste experience to the utmost,
to reach out eagerly and without fear for newer and richer experience."
Eleanor Roosevelt

When I started this project, I was scared and didn't know if I could do it well. If you know me and my personality, I like to strive for excellence. This is something I am still learning as a lifelong learner. A few years ago I discovered, it is okay to make mistakes as long as you learn from them, improve, and don't repeat them. It is important to improve each time you try something new. Although I consider myself a work in progress, this project helped me get out of my comfort zone. I want to thank my mentor Robbie Motter for this! You inspired me to write this book.

The role of a mentor is to empower, educate, and inspire you to accomplish whatever you want to accomplish. I believe we have a responsibility to pass along these same things, so consider me your mentor. If I have done my job well, I have empowered you, educated you by showing you things you haven't considered before. It is my hope that I have inspired you through my stories. BUT all of this would not be of any use unless you take action! I believed Robbie who impressed upon me to share my success and not keep it to myself. She was right when she said, "By sharing your successes you will enjoy them more and inspire others!" As you use principles you have learned by reading this book, share them with others, this will give you the enjoyment of investing in the success of many, not just your own.

If you asked me in early 2019 if writing a book is one of my goals, my answer would have been "no." I wanted a book, but I didn't think I could do it. Robbie, strategically empowered and inspired me to see other possibilities. She showed me I could achieve things beyond what I saw in front of me. Your mentors should stretch you beyond your current thinking. Robbie started by asking me to write a short paragraph, which she published in a local magazine. Then she asked some of the members of GSFE if we wanted to contribute to her book. I wanted to but had doubts if I could. She told us, "I will provide a book editor at no cost to you to review your story." I thought, *Why not? What do I have to lose?* I knew I needed to get out of my comfort zone and just do it! So I did.

When I was considering the goals for 2020, I knew I wanted to write a book to honor my parents as I am very grateful for the equipping, the sacrifices, and the love they passed on to me and my siblings. As I have met many people throughout my life whose parents didn't give them what my parents gave us. I have been even more grateful and felt so much love for all my parents provided for our family.

My life stories are a reflection of my parents' influence. I knew what they gave my siblings and I could be passed along through a book to help others with success in their lives. I had one problem I needed to solve, I knew I didn't write well. This is something I have known since grade school, writing is not one of my strengths. What does a person do when they want to accomplish a goal and they need to overcome a challenge to do it? They look for people who can help, who will help, and have the skills needed to get it done.

I learned so many things from writing this book. I had to put my own coaching philosophy to the test. That is, staying focused and having the discipline to do what was needed to be done. Because of that, I listed my goals with my coach, made a plan, and decided on a completion date. I needed to know when I was going to record, review, and approve each chapter.

I know from learning personal growth principles to get anything worthwhile done you need people who can help you. The great Jim Rohn said, "It takes a wise man to learn from his mistakes, but it is better to learn from the mistakes of others. It is best to learn from other's successes. It accelerates your own success." So, this book is to help you learn from my successes. My hope is you will create great success in your life, and overcome any excuses that could hold you back. That is what I did to write this book for you.

Often I hear people use the excuse of not having enough money. I also know, it's not usually a lack of money, it is the priority placed on their spending. It may also be limited thinking, our excuses can reveal our fears. Fear of failure, fear of rejection, even a fear of success worthiness.

Many years ago I found, when you have a budget and know your priorities, you will find a way. So when I made this goal, I looked into the cost and found the way in my budget. When I want something, I find out how much it costs, then I budget for it. It becomes a priority in my budget as I see the importance. I may choose to delay a purchase or do without something to get what I want. Many people don't know if they can afford something or not, so the unknown becomes an excuse. According to US Bank, in 2019, only 41% of American households follow a budget. Without a budget, how do you know you can or can't afford something. It comes back to priority.

Sometimes you can trade services with someone, and then is an investment of your time rather than your money. And if you trade something you are good at with someone that needs your talents, and you need theirs, it's a win-win to trade.

Many things we spend money on are not necessities or the basics, they are discretionary. When you look at your spending and reprioritize your purchases, you would be surprised at what you can get done. Often times you can afford things you once thought you couldn't.

So the perfect opportunity to write this book came during the 2020 COVID pandemic. With all of the restrictions, it gave me more time at home to focus on getting this book done. Remember FOCUS is Follow One Course Until Successful. It could have been more difficult with the distractions of everyday life, but with the mandated stay home order, I had more time. I was committed to dedicating time to get this book done in 2020 before the pandemic even came into the picture. It actually helped me accelerate my goal. My coach, Lori Raupe, and I looked at the available options, thinking outside the box and, when we couldn't meet in person we met via the internet, using Zoom.com to meet. This was actually a timesaver because we didn't have travel time. From the comfort of our homes, we worked on this book.

There are those who will use a pandemic, for example, as an excuse. There are others that can find a million other excuses, their minds are just wired that way. Our subconscious mind will "talk" ourselves out of things, that is just what it does, it goes for logic and previous programming. In fact, this includes me, I also find excuses not to get things done. The value a coach brings is having that other person encourage and empower you to keep moving forward.

What works for me is first deciding what I want to accomplish, then I set my priorities that include all that I want to get done. This is my system during this time of a pandemic, or at any other time. Of course, my priorities have shifted to accommodate the change in lifestyle and time flexibility in a time like this.

If you want to get something done, try using the S.M.A.R.T. system:

S is for Specific. What do I want to do as specific as I can make it? It doesn't work to be vague. What I want to do, and how I will get it done? At least the next few steps.

M is for Measurable. This should be the clarity around how you will know when you are a success. How I will know when I have reached my goal?

A is for Attainable. Can I see myself achieving this goal? I need to be honest with myself. At this point in my life, can I do this, and what are my responsibilities? I use my coach, and we decide what is achievable.

R is Relevant. Is this goal worthwhile, and is it aligned with my values? Is it a priority and how will I focus my attention to getting it done?

Finally the "T," is for Time-Bound, deciding a target date for completion. I provide a timeline when I want to complete each step in the process. This is very important. This is how I achieve my goals.

Yes, it is a challenge to do some things that are required in business to be successful. Networking for example, which I know is an important part of my business, but I don't use excuses I find ways. I look at the opportunities I do have, and we must shift with the times. So during this time, guess what? I have more time to record my stories for the book because I am not traveling to networking groups. I am working at home more, I have more time, and I set my priorities. My coach helped me with the planning, and encouragement, and focus. That is what they do. Has it been a challenge? Yes, of course, I was challenged. I have been frustrated and distracted by many things other than recording my stories. I have had mind blocks about what to record and write. With the personality I have, I love to be challenged,

I have learned to be coachable, and I also can stay focused when I need to be.

Believe it or not, I have enjoyed getting this book done because it is something I have wanted for a long time. I feel accomplished when I am doing and completing each step of the plan. When I can look back and see how much I have done, it brings me a high level of satisfaction.

Another thing I want to share with you. When this pandemic came into existence I used all that I had learned from my background working in crisis management. The number one thing is to be adaptable. My dogs taught me this lesson as well, they are very adaptable. They want to please their people so much, they show us that when you are adaptable you can make things happen. In contrast, you could stay stuck in crisis mode if you don't adapt and never move forward. My coach and I adopted our plan to write this book. Our original plan didn't work because we couldn't meet in person.

The second thing is to be prepared and use your common sense. We saw people stocking up on supplies, like bathroom tissue making it a crisis. If everyone was planning ahead this wouldn't have happened. I am a logical person, I use my common sense and I know this comes easier for me than some. But everyone can determine the next best thing to do based on their experience.

Next, I look for facts. This helped me as a microbiologist, and it helps me now. I don't listen to the mainstream news, negative journalisms, this feeds fear and your emotional response. That is not based on the facts. I go to the source of information. I look into the purpose of why information may be biased in one way or the other, like who is paying to get the information out to the people. The facts are the facts, these are found at a source that is as unbiased as possible. Science-based facts are the best place to start. I don't listen to the negative things, I focus on what I can do! What I do have, and what I can control.

I am a person who loves to challenge myself. My parents told me since I was little, I was stubborn even as a child and I would not give up. This can be a benefit, and also a detriment. The benefit is the determination, you want to get it done no matter what. It is a pride thing, the blindspots are not seeing the error in thinking, or negativity. Even when people give me advice, I don't always see that I am wrong, because I'm stubborn about it. When I look at why I feel I am right, I sometimes will be silently stubborn, and I will investigate what someone says on my own. I want to prove I am right, but if I find I am wrong, then I know I need to correct it. When I work with my mentor and I realize we all make mistakes and I'll need to work through these things. Yes, I like to be right, but at the same time I do make mistakes, and I need to admit it. I also learn from my mistakes, and I want to better myself. It is important not to beat yourself up when you discover these mistakes. It is okay to make mistakes, that is how we learn.

I look for things that have given me joy, like writing this book. I have learned to be adaptable and get out of my comfort zone. During this time we can find excuses, sure, but we can find solutions. Of course, it would be better in person. The human touch is important, and you can't do that online, so I have needed to find ways to touch people in other ways. So, I learned techniques to help, used technology. I made mistakes, I am a work in progress, I asked for help, I attended webinars, and asked people. I thought, *"Why not connect with people on Zoom? What do I have to lose?"* But I knew if we all stayed in isolation, it would not be healthy.

What is different? We don't meet at a restaurant to have meals together. We could do it if we want to. I just can't be in a negative place of making excuses or telling myself all of the reasons I can't do something. I must think of ways I can get things done. Personal development has helped me so much, my virtual mentors have helped me grow. I connect in ways that I might not have done otherwise. I call people, absolutely. I text people. I take pictures and text them to inform, encourage or connect with others. It is not how I did things before but I have found what does work. This has been a positive thing for me to have learned and continue learning ways to connect with technology. Before the pandemic, I didn't focus on the technology, because I was meeting them in person, which I like to do. It wasn't as important before, now it may be the "new norm" and I have embraced the change. I am learning new things in this time of the pandemic, this is always good for me. I don't make excuses. I hope you will be empowered to also embrace the change.

The training I received during my years in corporate life, you must be realistic and focus on what you can control. I like to be in control, maybe more than some. It is good to take charge and control the aspects of your life that you can control. I know I can't control others, which is a growth area for me. I know ultimately they must control themselves. I can only control myself. I work on not worrying about what I cannot control. I highly recommend you have a personal growth plan for yourself and be a life-long learner. You can control that! Manage what you can manage, and hope that the crisis gets over soon. Things have changed, and we will learn from it. What can we do to keep moving forward, rather than staying stuck in the past?

During this pandemic, I have really enjoyed spending more time with my dogs. As you already know I am a dog lover. I don't need to rush through walking the dogs. I can spend more time outside. And that exercise is so good for me since I have not been able to go to the gym. I have also been able to clean out my closets and get rid of things that I have been holding on to but didn't need any longer. I have wanted to do this for some time, but couldn't dedicate the time to do it.

I know, if you focus on sadness, you will be sad. If you focus on happiness, guess what? You will find happiness. Keep looking for the ways to find happiness, and get the things that are your priorities accomplished!

As I have gotten older, I have learned to appreciate my health, and for this, I am very grateful. This has been a focus and my number one priority. I have learned, it doesn't matter if you are a billionaire. if you don't have good health, you don't have anything. Look at Steve Jobs, with all of his money, he couldn't enjoy the end of his life. If you would take just this one piece of advice and put your health first even if it is a challenge. To me, this is worth everything. My philosophy is "Do the things you can control, let go of the things you can't control."

As you age or grow older, you appreciate things so much more. As I have grown older I see things differently. My goal is to help you, to inspire you to look for mentors and coaches to help you along the way. You can do whatever you set your mind to.

To parents, learn from how my parents raised me. The best thing you can do for your children is to love them unconditionally. Discipline is very important, even when they are very young, as soon as they understand you. When you set boundaries and guidelines, they will accept them. Do it with great love for them, they will understand, and they will appreciate it, especially when they get older. I observed my nephew discipline his son even at one year old, he understands what is expected. My parents knew this, and we are grateful for the way we were raised.

Don't get me wrong, when I was a teenager, sure I did rebel sometimes. According to my parents not that much, or as much as my other siblings. That was normal for teenagers, but I know my parents were loving and loved me unconditionally. This makes a big difference in kids growing up.

For those who are young and single, there is no such thing as getting too old to marry or to settle down. Be confident in this, marry when the time is right for you or you want to get married. I didn't marry until I was 48, this was my choice. It wasn't because I couldn't marry, or because I didn't have the opportunity to marry when I was younger. It was my choice. This is what was right for me.

You have a choice also, each of you will make different choices. Just own the things you do. I own everything I have done, good and bad. Sometimes it is hard to admit mistakes but own them anyway. I am so far from perfect, we will never be perfect because we are human and I am a work in progress. At my age now, I am enjoying my life and I am happy with who I am. This is what I want for you too, when you look back on your life, you know you did things to protect your health, and you own your choices with no regrets, be happy and contented.

Also, I've learned about personal development from my virtual mentors like John Maxwell, Darren Hardy, Jeff Olson, Jim Rohn, Tony Robbins. All of these people I have not met, except Jeff Olsen, I learned from them through reading their books and watching their videos. This is how I 'learned' from them and it is an affordable way to find mentors. This is an investment that is worthwhile, not an expense.

Moreover, I want this book to inspire, educate, and empower you, the reader! So writing a book I am able to influence and inspire, and empower more people. My goal is for you to find a mentor and or a coach to help you achieve your desires and passion and goals like I have done by writing this book with the help of my coach, Lori Raupe.

Success is when you enjoy the project and the work you do. This is a success for me. My life lessons are to feel content, excited, and proud. I look forward to sharing my life with others. I have learned to enjoy each moment.

Life Lessons: your reflection

A thought to inspire you:

"You never change your life until you step out of your comfort zone; change begins at the end of your comfort zone." Roy T. Bennett

What does this mean in your life? ....

....

....

....

Reflections to empower you:

What things in your life have you put off because you don't know how? ....

....

....

....

What goals are you working on, would it help you to make them SMART

Goals? ....

....

....

....

....

....

....

Have you used a mentor or a coach to help you accomplish something you know you need help with? ....

....

....

....

Reflections: what will you apply in your life? ....

....

....

....

....

....

....

....

....

....

....

....

....

"Strength doesn't come from what you can do.
It comes from overcoming the things you once thought you couldn't"

Angeline Benjamin

Acknowledgments

*If you talk about it, it is a dream, if you envision it, I
t is possible, but if you schedule it, it's real."*
Tony Robbins

I want to thank some people who have supported me and helped me make this book a reality. First, I want to thank my parents, they are in heaven now. Thank you, Mami and Papi, for your mentorship, guidance, and the discipline you taught me. I received from you my foundation in life. You showed me how to make decisions and to be responsible for my actions. You helped me know the difference between right and wrong and to be confident within myself. All parents want their kids to be that way, but you provided this for us. You also gave me your unconditional love.

Secondly, I want to thank Robbie Motter for her encouragement. She helped me look for ways to get this book done. With English as my second language, I needed help with writing. She asked me an important question, "What excuse is stopping you?" I realized my excuses were holding me back. Then she encouraged me to do it, "Find a way to do it." I made the decision to find a way through the referrals she gave me. Her message to all of us, "Don't let your age limit you, or your excuses limit you from accomplishing new things in life! She practices the messages to all of us!

I would also like to thank the many mentors in my life, mentors Joan Wakeland, who inspired me and her encouragement. Like me, she was an immigrant. She came from Jamaica, look for her book too! She has an incredible story. She told me I could do it!

Thank goodness for my writing coach, Lori Raupe. She has guided me in the process. Her encouragement and attention to my style helped me record this book. She supported me and listened to me, and saw the vision of how I wanted it written. This has been a great experience for me, I needed the discipline to get it done each month, so I could get it done by the deadline I set for myself.

If you are like me and not sure about doing something like writing a book, I want you to find someone like her to help you. Make sure they believe in you and ensure your book reflects what you want to share, and that will help you feel good! This will increase your confidence and help you know you can do it. Lori and I collaborated, sharing my stories with her, and with her skills and knowledge, we created this book. Within its pages are lessons from my life, so you can learn from me, my mistakes, and my successes. I recorded my stories for this book, which were then transcribed into a written form. It made what seemed impossible possible.

I would also like to thank Jackie Goldberg, The Pink Lady, for her book and how she lives her life encourages me to live my life to the fullest.

I want to thank Kelsey Ledford for her careful edit suggestions for the final manuscript of *Life Lessons Leading to Success*.

I also want to thank my husband, Mike, and my sisters, Indria and her husband Steve, Josie, Bernadette and her husband John, my brothers, Wendel, Johan and his wife Liena, my nieces, Mellisa and her husband Steve, Jessica, Monica, Kimberly, and my nephew Patrick and his wife Emma for their support and encouragement.

I would like to thank all my great teachers in high school, my inspiring professors in college and graduate school, Julia Stewart my mentor, Becky Stevens-Grobbelaar, my supervisor and coach, and all other managers and directors as coaches from the corporate world. I learned so much from them. Even when I heard people say, "I hate my boss!" I would ask them, "What would you do if you were in their place?" Many times when I reflected on this question and would think, *if I was in their shoes, I might have done the same things*. They weren't perfect. We are all human. And guess what? You aren't perfect, either. It isn't easy to be in the boss's shoes. Many bosses don't understand and don't work to support their subordinates, but you must appreciate the ones that did.

Lastly, I want to thank all my networking friends from Heart Link Laguna Niguel and GSFE for their encouragement. They are my cheerleaders.

References

http://agingcare.com Article about the aging and seniors.

https://high5test.com/strengthsfinder-free/

https://en.wikipedia.org/wiki/Enneagram_of_Personality

https://www.colorcode.com/media/whitepaper.pdf

https://wired2perform.com

https://www.theheartlinknetwork.com

https://www.globalsocietyforfemaleentrepreneurs.org

A portion of the proceeds from sales of this book will be given to non-profit organizations that adopt and train dogs for disabled persons.

About the Author

Angeline is an expert in goal setting, achievement, negotiation, and crisis management. She uses the skills learned from her corporate career with Hunt-Wesson Foods, Denny's, Nestle-Carnation, and Taco Bell Corporation. Her 28 years exemplary career In which the last 7 years she managed the Food Safety program covering all of the United States for Taco Bell Corporation. While in this capacity, she found her passion for coaching and training.

Angeline Benjamin is a motivational speaker delivering messages on personal development, leadership, cultural diversity, and confidence-building. As a coach, her approach is for her clients to focus their attention on getting massive action and results. Angeline believes in making a difference in people's lives through mentoring, coaching, and motivating audiences.

Angeline believes in helping people stay healthy and look their best. In 2013, she began her affiliation with Nerium, which grew to Neora, because she believes in their anti-aging products. Through this venture, she mentors others to stay healthy and feel good about themselves.

Angeline currently serves as the Director of The Global Society For Female Entrepreneurs (GSFE) of South Orange County Network and is Co-Director of the Menifee GSFE network. To continue empowering and inspiring all women, she partners with Big Media USA and having her podcast show called: "LIVE THE LIFE YOU WANT WITH GUSTO"

She is also a contributing author in a soon to be published book, "It's All About SHOWING UP and the POWER is in the ASKING."

Connect with Angeline, you can find her on LinkedIn, Facebook, AngelineBenjamin.com, or email her at: albenjamin.bb27@gmail.com

"The difference between who you are
and who you want to be is, the action you take."

Angeline Benjamin

Made in USA - Kendallville, IN
1202549_9798562541826
12.29.2020 1828